THE
WILD GAME
AND
FISH COOKBOOK

THE
WILD GAME
AND
FISH COOKBOOK

by Jim Bryant

Drawings by Lea Carmichael

LITTLE, BROWN AND COMPANY · BOSTON · TORONTO

COPYRIGHT © 1984 BY JIM BRYANT
ALL RIGHTS RESERVED. NO PART OF THIS BOOK MAY BE REPRODUCED IN ANY FORM OR BY ANY ELECTRONIC OR MECHANICAL MEANS INCLUDING INFORMATION STORAGE AND RETRIEVAL SYSTEMS WITHOUT PERMISSION IN WRITING FROM THE PUBLISHER, EXCEPT BY A REVIEWER WHO MAY QUOTE BRIEF PASSAGES IN A REVIEW.

FIRST EDITION

Library of Congress Cataloging in Publication Data

Bryant, Jim.
　The wild game and fish cookbook.

　Includes index.
　1. Cookery (Game)　2. Cookery (Fish)　I. Title.
TX751.B78　1983　　641.6'91　　83-16217
ISBN 0-316-11327-1

VB

Designed by Dede Cummings

*Published simultaneously in Canada
by Little, Brown & Company (Canada) Limited*

PRINTED IN THE UNITED STATES OF AMERICA

ontents

Preface xv

PART ONE:
PREPARING WILD GAME AND FISH

Preliminary Rules 3
  How to Select Game 5
    Wild Duck 5
    Wild Goose 5
    Pigeon 5
    Squab 5
    Wild Turkey 6
    Game Birds 6
    Rabbit 6
    Venison 6
Dressing and Skinning Game 7
    Opossum or Possum 7
    Squirrel 7
    Rabbit 8
    Bear 9
    Raccoon or Coon 9
    Deer 10

Preparing Wild Birds	13
Plucking	13
Drawing	14
Cooking	15
Wild Duck	15
Wild Goose	15
Dove	16
Pheasant	16
Partridge	16
Squab and Pigeon	17
Quail	17
Preparing Fish	18
Cleaning Fish	18
Crayfish or Crawfish	19
Bullfrog	19
Mussels	20
Freshwater Snapping Turtle	20
Carving Techniques for Wild Game and Fish	22
Fish	22
Meat	22
Rib Roast	23
Roast Game Birds	24
Boiled Game Birds	24
Broiled Game Birds	24
Duck and Goose	24
Cooking Methods for Game and Game Birds	25
Roasting	25
Broiling	25
Stewing	26
Frying	26
Cooking Methods for Fish	28
Sautéing	28
Frying	28
Broiling	29

Boiling	29
Baking	29
Corning	30
Smoking and Drying Techniques	31
Smoking Fish	31
Preparing Fish for the Smoker	32
Smoking Instructions	33
Smoking Meat	33
Smoked Wild Turkey	33
Smoked Goose	34
Smoked Quail	34
Smoked Ham	35
Smoked Wild Boar Sausage	35
Drying Meat	36

PART TWO: RECIPES

Venison	41
Roast Saddle of Venison	41
Tangy Roast Haunch of Venison	42
Apple Cider Venison Roast	42
Apple Valley Venison Roast	43
Venison Pot Roast	44
Herbed Venison and Mushrooms	44
Venison Cutlet Casserole	46
Venison Cutlet with Apple	46
Broiled Venison with Corbin Steak Sauce	47
Broiled Venison Steak with Garlic Sauce	48
Venison Steak with Wine Sauce	48
Venison Chops in Wine	49
Country-Style Venison	50
Bryant County Venison	51
Venison Casserole Claret	52
Sunset Venison Stew	53
Orange Venison Stew	54
Barbecued Venison Kabobs	54
Venison Meatballs and Wine Sauce	55

Uncle Herbert's Secret Venison Chili ... 56
Pine Mountain Venison Chili and Beans ... 56
Grandma's Venisonburgers ... 57
Venison Meatloaf ... 58
Venison Sausage ... 58
Venison Tongue ... 59
Venison Tongue Wine Sauce ... 59
Venison Tongue Tangy Sauce ... 60
Sautéed Venison Liver with Apple Slices ... 60

Bear ... 61

Bear Steak Rollups ... 61
Bear Hot Pot ... 62
Rolled Bear Steak Loaf ... 63
Bear Cubes in Wine Sauce ... 64

Raccoon ... 65

Cumberland Valley Coon ... 65
Marinated Coon ... 66

Possum ... 67

Possum with Brandy and Wine Sauce ... 67
Southern Baked Possum ... 68

Rabbit ... 69

Kentucky Rabbit ... 69
Pan-Fried Rabbit with Country Colonel Gravy ... 70
Rabbit with Mushroom Sauce ... 70
Lemon-Broiled Rabbit ... 71
Rabbit in Wine Sauce ... 72
Sage Rabbit ... 72
Hot Spiced Rabbit ... 73
The Colonel's Favorite Rabbit Recipe ... 74
Oven-Fried Sesame Rabbit ... 74
Coriander Rabbit and Wild Rice ... 75
Crusty Oven-Fried Rabbit ... 76
Italian Rabbit with Almonds ... 76
Rabbit and Cheese Casserole ... 77
Lemon-Baked Rabbit ... 78
Brunswick Stew ... 79

Squirrel	80
Mountain Fried Squirrel and Gravy	80
Squirrel in Orange and Honey Sauce	81
Curried Squirrel and Rice	82
Lemon-Fried Squirrel	83
Squirrel in Orange Sauce	84
Squirrel in Wine Sauce	84
Herb-Fried Squirrel	85
Tasty Squirrel Casserole	86
Squirrel Chowder	86
Groundhog	88
Braised Groundhog and Bourbon Sauce	88
Garlic-Flavored Fried Groundhog	90
Wild Turkey	93
Roast Wild Turkey	93
Wild Turkey Dressing	94
Giblet Gravy	94
Currant-Glazed Wild Turkey	96
Simple Broiled Wild Turkey	97
Smoked Turkey and Rice with Pineapple Sauce	98
Wild Duck	99
Wine and Bourbon Duck	100
Roast Wild Duck with Herbs	101
Lemon-Roast Wild Duck	102
Bloody Wild Duck with Orange Sauce	103
Orange-Glazed Wild Duck	104
Duck Breast in Wine Sauce	104
Herb-Fried Wild Duck	105
Barbecued Wild Duck Breast	106
Kentucky-Style Wild Duck	106
Wild Duck Pâté	107
Wild Duck Tidbits and Rice with Sauce	108
Wild Goose	109
Goose with Fruit Stuffing	109
Roast Goose	110
Fricasseed Goose	111
Goose Cracklings	112

Pheasant 113
    Barbecued Marinated Pheasant 113
    Raisin-and-Pecan-Stuffed Pheasant 114
    Roast Pheasant with Vegetables 115
    Pheasant Breast with Mushroom Sauce 116

Quail and Other Small Game Birds 117
    Roast Quail 117
    Kentucky Stuffed Quail with Cream Sauce 118
    Quail Supreme 120
    Quail Sauterne 121
    Grandma Rosa's Stuffed Quail with Tomato Sauce 122
    Famous Old-Style Quail 124
    Little Deviled Birds 125
    Quail Potpie 126
    Bluegrass Quail with Wine Sauce 127
    Quail with Yellow Rice 128
    Bryant County Quail 128
    Quail Pâté 129
    Quail Liver Pâté 129
    Hearty Quail Stew 130
    Smoked Quail Salad 131
    Open-Faced Quail Sandwich 132
    Baked Dove and Cashew Gravy 132
    Dove and Gravy 134
    Potted Pigeon 134
    Mountain Laurel Squab 135
    Sherried Ptarmigan with Pecan Dressing 136
    Ptarmigan with Orange Glaze 137
    Almond-Stuffed Woodcock 138
    Braised Woodcock 139
    Barbecued Sage Grouse 140
    Breast of Grouse 140
    Grouse with Almond and Wine Sauce 142
    Woodbine Roast Partridge 143

Stuffing for Game Birds 144
    Sausage Stuffing 144
    Chestnut and Currant Stuffing 144

Rice-Raisin-Almond Stuffing	145
Corn Bread Stuffing	146
Bread Stuffing	147

Fish and Shellfish — 151

Cheesy Trout Deluxe	151
Baked Trout in Wine Sauce	152
Herb-Stuffed Salmon	152
Baked Salmon	154
Melanie Suzanne's Stuffed Salmon	154
Boiled Salmon with Tart Sauce	155
Crispy Lake Bass	156
Wine-Baked Striped Bass Fillets	156
Beer-Fried Bass	157
Savory Baked Striped Bass with Piquant Sauce	158
Baked Bluegill	159
Fish and Chips	160
Almond-Baked Fish Fillets	162
Poached Fish Fillets	162
Stuffed Walleyed Pike	163
Skipper's Baked Bluefish	164
Spicy Baked King Mackerel	164
Old Irish Fish Casserole	165
Cumberland Mountain Fried Crappie	166
Broiled Spicy Flounder	167
Flounder with Wine Sauce	168
Fried Catfish	168
Baked Catfish	169
Creamy Crayfish Casserole	170
Old Kentucky Creamed Crayfish	171
Sherried Mussels and Crayfish with Brandy Sauce	172
Pan-Fried Mussels	173
Deep-Fried Mussels	173
Oven-Fried Mussels	174
Mussel Fritters	174
Mussel Fricassee	175
Mountain Mussel Soup	175
Clam Chowder	176

Frogs' Legs, Turtle, and Rattlesnake	177
Crispy Frogs' Legs	177
Fancy Baked Frogs' Legs	178
Frogs' Legs and Sausage	178
Turtle Fricassee with Wine	179
Fried Succulent Snapper	180
Camp Town Turtle Soup	180
Tennessee Turtle Soup	182
Cumberland Mountain Terrapin	182
Kentucky Terrapin	184
Rattlesnake Fillets	184
Savory Rattlesnake and Browned Duck Liver	185
Sautéed Rattlesnake Steaks	186
Flambéed Rattlesnake	186
Rattlesnake Delight	187
Rattlesnake Cocktail	187
Favorite Accompaniments	188
Old-Time Hardtack	188
Baking Powder Biscuits	189
Buttermilk Biscuits	189
Whole Wheat Biscuits	190
Potato Biscuits	190
Crackling Bread	191
Country Corn Bread	191
Pawpaw Muffins	192
Jennifer's Hush Puppies	192
Old-Time Corn Fritters	193
Granny's Egg Bread	193
Home-Fried Potatoes	194
Poke Sallet	194
Fried Green Tomatoes	195
Shuck Beans	195
Spinach Salad	196
Appendixes	197
Herbs and Spices to Use with Wild Game and Fish	197
Oven Temperatures	198

Standard Measurements	198
Sizes of Cans	198
Cooking Terms and Definitions	199
Index	203

reface

THIS BOOK IS FOR PEOPLE who take up the rod or gun and want to learn how to slaughter, skin, and dress their catch. It covers large and small game and describes techniques for selecting and preparing wild game, carving, and smoking.

It tells how to cook venison, rabbit, possum, quail, squirrel, and many other game animals. Some recipes are old family treasures that have never before been printed; others are standard rules that have stood the test of years and still head their respective lists.

Modern people care about the nutritional composition of the food they eat. They want to know the fat content, number of calories it contains, protein, the amounts of fat, sugar, and added preservatives, and so on. Nutritionally, wild game and fish are among the best sources of food; they are high in protein and low in calories and cholesterol. Wild game and fish are widely available and free for the taking. So enjoy them when you can. They taste good and are healthy for you — not to mention savings on grocery bills.

PART ONE

PREPARING WILD GAME AND FISH

reliminary Rules

HUNTERS AND FISHERMEN should live by commonsense rules to assure the best results in preparing their catch for the table.

Take care to prevent game meat from becoming tainted. Certain species should not be allowed to come in contact with the sebaceous gland, musk glands, internal fluid, or body excreta. Coagulated blood in muscular tissue and body temperature also play an important part in spoilage. Immediately after the kill, if possible, cut the animal's jugular vein, execute a fast, clean job of dressing the carcass, and store it in a cool place.

Always be prepared to field-dress an animal or fish. Take along sharp knives, kitchen shears, sealable plastic bags, and larger bags in which to carry the total catch.

Be sure to cut out all areas where blood has collected from wounds and to remove all shot. If you overlook a shot or two, someone may bite down on it later and spoil his or her meal.

Soak game in a solution of water, baking soda, and salt. (For each gallon of water, add 2 tablespoons of baking soda and 4 tablespoons of salt.) Let stand in refrigerator overnight to eliminate any wild taste that may remain.

The most practical and easiest way to deal with cleaning and dressing wild game in preparation for cooking is to turn the task over to a local commercial firm that specializes in dressing meat for the market. However, you must bleed the carcass in the field immediately after the kill and take it directly to the butcher.

ow to Select Game

Wild Duck

Ducks should be soft to the touch. A large mallard serves 3 people and a small teal serves 1 person. Allow 1 pound per person.

Wild Goose

A goose should have a pliable, yellow bill and soft, fat, yellow feet. A green goose is a young native goose. A 10-pound goose serves 8 or more people. Allow 1 to 1½ pounds per person.

Pigeon

Pigeons should be plump. Allow 1 small or ½ large pigeon per person.

Squab

Squabs, young pigeons that have never been allowed to fly, should also be plump. Allow 1 squab per person.

Wild Turkey

A turkey should have smooth feathers, and soft, pliable cartilage at end of the breastbone. Allow ½ to 1 pound per person.

Game Birds

Game birds, such as quail, grouse, ptarmigan, and so on, should have soft feet and pliable bills. Allow 1 bird per person.

Rabbit

Young rabbits with soft ears and paws, short necks, and smooth, sharp claws are best. Allow 1 rabbit per 2 or 3 people.

Venison

Venison should hang two weeks or longer, according to taste, before preparation. Fat should be white and firm. Arrangements for hanging can be made with your butcher.

ressing and Skinning Game

OPOSSUM OR POSSUM

Bleed possum immediately after the kill, as for all other game. Cut the jugular vein and hang the possum by its tail. Scald the possum in boiling water containing ½ cup of lime, being careful not to overscald. Submerge the carcass for about 20 seconds — just long enough to loosen the hairs — then scrape off all the hair with a large, dull knife. Make a short cut in the belly parallel to the backbone; gut the carcass and remove the musk glands under the forearms. Remove the head, feet, and tail. Soak the meat in 1 gallon water, 2 tablespoons baking soda, and 4 tablespoons salt solution and let stand in refrigerator overnight.

SQUIRREL

To skin a squirrel the quick way, make a cut across the lower back, insert the fingers of both hands, and pull both ways. The pelt can be removed from stem to stern in one swift motion.

Make a short cut in the belly parallel to the backbone; then gut the carcass.

A squirrel is usually cut into six pieces — four legs, rib cage, and loin. To cut a squirrel into sections first remove the legs, then separate the ribs and back section by cutting vertically up the squirrel's sides.

Rabbit

It is best to wear rubber gloves when dressing a rabbit, because it may have tularemia, better known as rabbit fever. If its liver shows white or yellow spots, the rabbit most likely has the fever and should be buried deeply enough in a hole that dogs will not be able to dig it up. Absence of disease is very important, but don't worry about germs that may lurk in rabbit pieces; they will be killed in the cooking process or at below-freezing temperatures when the meat has been stored in a freezer.

It is best to field-dress a rabbit as soon as you kill it to prevent the possibility of meat becoming tainted, but many hunters wait until they get home to do the job. That is acceptable only if the time lapse between the kill and dressing is short and the carcass is kept cool.

To skin a rabbit, make a cut across the middle of the back, insert the fingers of both hands, and pull both ways. Lift the legs out of the pelt, snip off the forepaws and hindpaws, and then remove the head.

Butchering a rabbit is a simple process — it should be cut up much the same way squirrels are, in six pieces. First, remove the hind legs from the back. Then cut the main part of the back with the thick saddle away from the upper back at the lowest ribs. Next, cut along the backbone, dividing the ribs and the forelegs into serving pieces. Finally, rinse the pieces thoroughly with water, removing blood and other contamination, such as dirt and hair. If the rabbit is not to be prepared right away, place it in water, baking soda, and salt solution and let stand in refrigerator.

A rabbit that is not young and tender should be parboiled. Place pieces in a pot with two tablespoons of salt in water to cover and boil until tender. The meat should puncture easily when pierced with a fork.

Bear

Cut the jugular vein and bleed; then remove the head. Cut the hide down the middle underside from the neck to the back legs, between the hide and flesh. Turn the bear from side to side until hide is removed. Use a meat cleaver and remove the legs below the knees; then cut through the breastbone and between the buttocks to the backbone. Remove the insides, by cutting the end of the large intestine and stripping out. The meat is cut up much the same way as hogs are. Separate the meat as you would in slaughtering a hog, cutting on either side of the backbone. Cut out the shoulders and hams for curing in salt, and the flank, neck, and lower part of the shoulder for small stewing pieces.

In most cases bear meat has to be parboiled to gain tenderness. Parboil for 20 minutes per pound plus 20 minutes more. The water should be boiling, 212 degrees, when meat is added, after which the temperature will drop to 135 degrees. Cook over medium heat until water starts to bubble very gently, which will indicate that the right temperature has been reached. Lower heat to maintain bubbling. Be careful not to overcook.

Raccoon or Coon

After killing a coon it is best to cut its jugular vein and bleed it as soon as possible to prevent spoilage and make an easier job of butchering. After this is done the coon is ready to be skinned.

Follow this simple procedure if you want to save the prized pelt: First, cut around all four legs at the foot joint. Cut the pelt on the inside middle of both hind legs from rings to the crotch. Do the same with the front legs to the chest. Cut up the middle from the crotch to the chest and up to the bottom jaw. Cut around the tail on the underside only. Connect cuts. Skin out both hind legs, make a small cut between bone and tendon of the hind legs, and insert a gambrel stick. Starting at the base of the tail, use two small sticks, gripping them together firmly over the tail, and pull carefully. The tail fur should come off the bone easily. Exercise care not to pull the tail bone off because it would ruin the pelt. Pull the pelt off the front legs, carefully cutting the mesentery (membranes) between the skin and muscle at times. Cut up the front legs and skin them out. Remove the pear-shaped glands under the forearms. Skin around the neck up to the head. Carefully cut off the ears even with the head; a bad cut reduces the value of the pelt. Skin around the eyes, leaving only the eyeballs. Go down the nose, cutting off the end so that the nose button is still attached to the pelt. Then cut the flesh down the middle from the throat to the crotch and remove the internal organs. Remove the head, feet, and tail. Soak the carcass in water, baking powder, and salt solution and let stand in refrigerator overnight before cooking.

DEER

These instructions for deer also apply to caribou, moose, elk, antelope, and other large game of this category.

Before skinning and dressing a deer or any other carcass, you must be prepared for the job. You will need a long butcher knife, a meat cleaver, a boning knife, and a butcher's saw or hacksaw.

First, hang up the carcass by the hind legs, using meat hooks or a gambrel stick. Next, remove the scent glands on the hind legs at the inside of the knee joint; then remove the testes. Cut around the hind legs just below the knee joint. Cut down the inside of each leg, the two cuts meeting at the crotch. Cut around both front legs and cut down the inside of each leg, the two cuts meeting at the chest. Make a cut from the crotch to the chest, connecting both leg cuts.

Start at the back legs and peel off the hide down to the base of the neck. At this point you must take special care if you want to have the head mounted for your trophy room. Make a cut along the back of the neck, not the underside, from the shoulders to between the ears. Then cut straight down the front to the lowest point on the brisket and continue cutting completely around the animal. Carefully peel off the hide from the shoulders and neck and remove the back section hide.

Cut the flesh where the skull joins the neck and twist off the head. At this point remove the tongue — it's edible too. Give the hide and exposed part of the skull a generous salting and take it to a taxidermist.

Cut down between the hams with a meat cleaver. Then use a butcher knife to cut from the hams to the chest. Separate the ribs with the meat cleaver. Again using the butcher knife, cut down the brisket, then around the anus. Now remove the insides. Save the liver if you like.

The best ways to prepare venison are:

Neck — Put through food chopper for hamburger or stew

Shoulder — Bone and tie and marinate — or leave plain — for roasting, pot roasting, or stewing, or put through food chopper

Loin — Broiled steaks, roast, or chops

Ribs — Cut into chops or spare ribs

Flank — Marinate or leave plain for stewing, or put through food chopper

Top hindquarter — Steaks

Lower hindquarter — Roast

Shank — Stew or hamburger

Liver, brains, and tongue — Prepare as from domesticated animals

Cooking Venison Old venison requires long cooking or parboiling, but if it is young and properly prepared it will make excellent eating. If you have never tasted venison before, you are in for a surprise; it tastes better than beef. However, you should take special precautions not to overcook it. Venison steaks are best prepared rare to medium rare; overcooking toughens the meat.

Parboiling Venison   Parboiling makes meat tender and removes any wild taste that may remain. Simply place meat in pot, add water to cover; mix in salt, red and black pepper, and some crushed garlic cloves if desired. Boil meat until tender. The meat should puncture easily when pierced with a fork.

Preparing Wild Birds

THE DECISION TO SKIN or not to skin any bird may make the difference between a tasty flavor and a mediocre one. I prefer the skin left on because much of the fat and flavor lie just under the skin; the skin helps hold in the juices and keeps the meat tender and moist, adding to the final flavor and succulence of the cooked bird.

Some people choose to skin thin-skinned birds such as quail, sage grouse, forest grouse, and pheasant without plucking the feathers, removing skin and feathers in one simple operation.

Birds should be cleaned and dressed as soon as possible after they are killed. The operation is easier and the chance of meat becoming tainted is lessened. With this in mind most hunters field-dress their game rather than wait to do the job at home.

If you decide to dress your birds at home you should first prepare your work area. Be sure to spread lots of newspapers to catch the feathers and other discarded parts. Rubber gloves may prove useful and a plastic garbage bag should be kept nearby for disposal of feathers and intestines wrapped in newspapers.

PLUCKING

One method for removing feathers is the old-fashioned one — dipping the birds in scalding water, then plucking out the feathers.

Leave the birds in the hot water just long enough to loosen the feathers so they may be removed easily.

It is preferable to do this task out of doors. You will need a washtub three-quarters full of water — fill it with a garden hose — resting on rocks with a hot wood fire. Heat the water to about 145 degrees.

Grasp the bird by the legs and lower it into the hot water until all of the feathered area is submerged; leave it in just long enough to loosen the feathers without cooking the meat (about 20 seconds). Overscalding causes the skin to break.

First pluck out the large feathers — the pinion feathers in the wings and the tail feathers. Pull out the feathers in the direction in which they grow; otherwise you may tear the skin, unless the bird is old and tough.

After you remove the feathers and down, there may still be a fuzz, called pinfeathers, left on the skin. Pinfeathers or new growth may be removed with a small knife or by singeing — passing the bird through a flame or holding a torch close to it.

ꙮ DRAWING

When you have completed the task of removing the feathers, it is time to remove the internal organs. Make an incision in the skin just below the breastbone and remove the inner organs, being very careful not to break the gall bag attached to the liver, to prevent the parts with which it comes in contact from becoming bitter. Save the gizzard, liver, and heart, along with the neck, for broth.

After the birds are dressed, wash them thoroughly with cold water and clean inside and out. Remove the head (if you have not already done so) and the feet up to the drumstick joint.

The most practical and easiest method for dealing with plucking, drawing, and dressing game birds is to turn the task over to a commercial firm that specializes in dressing poultry for the market.

COOKING

The first step to take before cooking is to soak the birds in a water, baking soda, and salt solution and let stand in the refrigerator overnight to eliminate any remaining wild taste.

Properly prepared wild birds can be a delicacy; if you haven't tried one you're in for a treat.

For the best results in cooking game birds, use proven recipes such as those in this book. With so many different recipes, one may become your favorite, but you will enjoy all of them.

WILD DUCK

Wild ducks are classified in three sizes: a large wild duck, such as a mallard, weighs 3 to 4 pounds; a medium, 2 to 3 pounds; and a small one, about 1½ to 2 pounds.

Ducks may be roasted at a high temperature for about 30 minutes and served very rare, or at lower temperatures for about 2 to 4 hours. Strips of bacon or salt pork can be laid across the duck's breast to keep it moist during the roasting period. Wild ducks should never be stuffed.

If you think the only way to prepare wild duck is to bake it, you are in for a surprise. Wild ducks may also be stewed with turnips or cabbage, used in gumbos, fried highly seasoned, or cooked in casseroles, to mention only a few ways.

WILD GOOSE

Geese range in size from a small cackling goose (3 to 4 pounds), a medium lesser Canada goose (4 to 6 pounds), and a large Canada goose (up to 10 pounds). The latter is the most prized for its superb flavor.

Most geese are old; their meat is tougher than that of other birds, and they require parboiling to make them tender. Parboiling usually cuts baking time in half. Bake parboiled geese at 350 degrees for 15 minutes per pound. If geese have not been parboiled, bake for 30 minutes per pound.

A goose is a very fatty bird. Some cooks remove the excess fat by piercing the breast and thighs with a two-tined fork and roasting for 1 hour, on a rack, in a 375-degree oven. This allows a great deal of undesired fat to be eliminated and discarded from the goose before it is served.

Dove

Doves, considered a tasty treat, are prized the world over. They are abundant throughout North America. Doves weigh about 6 ounces.

Braising is the most common cooking method for doves, but many people favor roasting.

Pheasant

Older pheasants, as other birds, usually have to be parboiled; the younger ones make the best eating. A pheasant's age is determined by the shape of its wing tip; young ones are short and rounded, older ones longer and sharp pointed.

The average weight of a pheasant is 2½ to 3 pounds.

Partridge

Partridge less than a year old are good roasted. Older ones are best prepared in casseroles or braised.

The average weight of a Hungarian partridge is 12 to 13 ounces; a chukar partridge weighs 18 to 20 ounces.

Squab and Pigeon

A squab is a young pigeon whose tender meat makes excellent eating. Roast squab are great.

A pigeon is best prepared in a casserole, but it can also be stuffed and roasted. A pigeon's flavor depends mainly on its diet or the region it comes from.

Quail

The size of quail is often wrongly related to the tenderness of their meat; it is not true that the smaller the bird the more tender. Quail are usually tougher than their size may indicate.

Some people prefer to skin a quail, removing feathers and skin in one operation. Although this is a quick method for removing the feathers, it robs the bird of extra flavor.

Quail are excellent prepared almost any way, but braising is the most popular method.

Quail range in size from a small bobwhite quail, 4 to 6 ounces, to a large mountain quail, 9 to 16 ounces; they are found throughout North America.

reparing Fish

☙ CLEANING FISH

All fish must be cleaned before cooking by various methods. They can be scaled, skinned, and filleted. Fresh fish should never be allowed to dry out before scaling. Dryness makes the scales difficult to remove.

Many types of fish scalers are on the market; all are good, but a knife blade can do just as good a job. A scraping motion from the tail forward to the head is the normal procedure for removing scales.

There are many ways to prepare fish. Size is an important factor that determines whether fish is filleted, cut up, or cooked whole. Large fish may be left whole for baking or cut into pieces for frying, broiling, or boiling. A large salmon may be cut into slices and cooked as steaks. Small fish, with their eyes removed, are usually cooked whole.

Filleting, the simplest and quickest procedure, is the most popular method for preparing fish. Starting with a whole fish, scale it, but do not bother to gut it. Use a sharp fillet knife and cut down vertically behind the gill plate to the backbone, then turn the knife horizontally and follow the backbone closely all the way to the tail.

The skin is usually left on the fillets to hold the meat together during cooking, but may be removed from firmer fish if desired. To remove the skin, hold the fillet tail with one hand, then with the other hand use the fillet knife, starting at the tail, and cut in a forward sawing motion until the meat is separated from the skin.

CRAYFISH OR CRAWFISH

Crayfish are small freshwater crustaceans that are closely related to the lobster; they seldom grow larger than 6 inches long. They are found throughout the United States, in rivers and streams, and on every continent except Africa. Many people find crayfish a delicacy, but some have never seen, let alone eaten, one. In some parts of the States crayfish are referred to as crawfish, and in Kentucky, Virginia, and Tennessee they are called crawdads.

Cleaning and Shelling Crayfish   Only the tail meat of the crayfish is edible. Remove the meat by taking the front half of the body between thumb and index finger of one hand and the tail section between thumb and index finger of the other hand, then separating the tail by pinching or pulling apart. Peel off the shell and legs with fingers. Cut along the outside of the tail meat and remove the black line (the intestine).

Boiling Crayfish   Drop cleaned crayfish tail meat into boiling water to which salt has been added; boil for 20 minutes, then remove and plunge into cold water.

Sautéed Crayfish   Sauté lightly in melted butter for about 5 to 10 minutes. Serve with butter poured over and a hot sauce or catsup. Great at parties or luncheons.

BULLFROG

Cleaning and Dressing   Cut the skin all the way around the belly and back with a sharp knife. Peel the skin down and off the legs with pliers. Using kitchen shears, separate the legs from the body and remove the bottom joint of the legs with the feet and discard. Rinse thoroughly with cold running water and pat dry with paper towels.

Soaking Place clean frogs' legs in a stainless-steel or porcelain bowl and add milk to cover; soak for about 2 hours before cooking. Soaking tenderizes the frogs' legs.

Another method is to soak the frogs' legs for 10 to 20 minutes in 1 quart of water into which ½ cup of white vinegar has been added.

Mussels

Mussels — found in freshwater streams and lakes in many parts of the United States — are mollusks (shellfish) and belong to the family of clams and oysters. Properly prepared, they are a great food.

Cleaning Mussels Mussels must be cleaned very carefully to remove as much sand as possible from their insides. Scrub each one with a rough brush under cold running water. With a knife, scrape off the small hairs or beards that stick out from one side of the closed shell halves. Place the mussels in fresh water for 1 to 2 hours before cooking to let them disgorge their sand and lose some of their saltiness. Just before cooking, wash and drain the mussels again.

Shelling Mussels Boil a small amount of water. Place the mussels in a pot and steam for about 5 minutes or until the shells pop open.

Freshwater Snapping Turtle

Most snapping turtles weigh 10 to 20 pounds undressed, but 35-pounders are not unheard of. Older turtles sometimes weigh 50 to

60 pounds. The alligator snapper, found in the lower Mississippi River and its bayous, tips the scales at 140 pounds.

Turtle meat is of seven different types and flavors. Like chicken, some of the meat is dark and some is light. Many people consider turtle meat a delicacy and well worth the extra effort it takes to catch it. The meat can be prepared many ways, but is usually fried or used in soup.

Cleaning Snapping Turtle or Terrapin The first step in cleaning a turtle is to cut off its head. This may be accomplished by grasping its extended head with pliers held in one hand and, using a knife held in the other hand, to cut through the neck. Tie a heavy cord to the turtle's tail and hang it up to bleed for 10 to 15 minutes.

Next, plunge the turtle into boiling water and boil for 5 minutes. Lift the turtle out of the water and let it cool off. Then lay the carcass on its back and, using a sharp knife, cut under the upper shell and lift it off; repeat the procedure with the lower one. Cut open the turtle and remove the entrails and gall bag, being careful not to rupture the gall bag because its fluid makes the meat taste bitter; remove the eggs and liver and reserve them for other recipes. Skin the neck, legs, and tail and remove them from the body; place these and other cut-up pieces in 1 gallon of water, to which has been added 2 tablespoons of baking soda and 4 tablespoons of salt; let stand in refrigerator overnight.

Carving Techniques for Wild Game and Fish

THREE THINGS ARE ESSENTIAL to good carving: first, knowledge of the anatomy of the game animal, game bird, or fish to be served; second, a sharp carving knife; and third, acquaintance with the choice portions of the particular dish that is to be prepared.

Fish

In preparing fish, be careful not to break the flakes. With such fish as haddock, cod, and flounder, run the knife down the full length of the back fin to separate the flesh from the bone. Portions can then be divided easily.

Be sure to serve salmon with a little of the thick and a little of the thin flesh to each person. The middle of a fish is usually the choicest in flavor, the tail part the most tasteless.

When you fry such fish as flounder or sole, it is wiser to fillet them — that is, remove the bone — before frying, as they are easier to serve so prepared.

Meat

Because they lack a compact form, some cuts of meat should be tied, skewered, or sewn into shape before cooking. Use white string when tying; use steel skewers in preference to wooden ones when skewering; and use a trussing needle threaded with fine white string when sewing. You can secure the meat by any of these methods.

Serve gravy in a separate vessel to make the carver's work easier.

Rib Roast

When the bone is left in a rib roast, cut the meat in long, thin slices from the thin to the thick end. The thick, round muscle is the choice portion of the roast, the meat at the thin end being more or less tough as well as containing excess fat. It is wiser to remove the greater part of the thin end and cook it in another way than roasting so it can be used to greater advantage.

When the bone has been removed from a rib roast and the meat tied, skewered, or sewn into shape, cut thin slices across the upper surface. Leave the skewers or tie threads in place until the meat is cold so that it will retain its shape.

Roast Game Birds

First remove the leg, then the wing, next the side bones. Cut thin slices, running from the head toward the tail, from the breast. Cut off the wishbone and make a crosswise incision in the body of the bird to remove the dressing if the bird has been stuffed. In a larger bird whose tendons have been removed from the leg before cooking, this portion should be as tender as any other. If the tendons have not been removed, it is better to cook these parts further to make them tender.

Boiled Game Birds

Carve in the same manner, except for the breast, which should be cut into thick slices. No dressing is served with boiled birds.

Broiled Game Birds

Split down the back before cooking; at serving time, cut lengthwise through the breastbone, and, if the bird is large, into quarters, cutting across the breastbone. If the birds are small, serve a whole one to each person.

Duck and Goose

Carve these in almost the same manner as other birds; the breast, however, is not so thick, and the leg and wing joints lie somewhat closer to the body. The breast and wings of these birds are the choicest portions; the legs are generally reserved and deviled, or reheated in some other way. The legs of a flying bird and the wings of a swimmer are, with the breast, the choicest portions.

Cooking Methods for Game and Game Birds

ROASTING

First, wipe with a damp cloth, then skewer and tie if necessary to keep the meat in shape. For deer, moose, and elk allow 12 minutes for each pound plus 15 minutes extra; for bear, 20 minutes to the pound and 20 minutes extra. These close-grained meats are indigestible unless they are well cooked, but take care not to overcook. Some cooks flour meat before roasting.

As the object in roasting is to keep the juices within the meat, it is necessary to apply intense heat at first, to sear the outside and form a firm coating through which the juices cannot escape. Therefore, when roasting, have the oven sufficiently hot when the meat goes in. Reduce the heat after 20 minutes of roasting at high temperatures. Baste frequently with the fat that accumulates in the pan, to prevent the outside from burning or drying out. You may also dredge the meat or sprinkle it once or twice with flour and salt. Some cooks use covered roasting pans or baking bags, claiming that method keeps the meat moister and eliminates the work of basting.

BROILING

Broiling is much like roasting, except that it is used for smaller pieces of meat, only choice portions being suitable for this method of cooking. The fire must be hot, the object being, as in roasting, to keep the juices in the meat; therefore, it is necessary to sear the outside quickly. In broiling, the meat should be moved a little farther from the source of heat, and the cooking should proceed more slowly. The broiling pan should be slightly greased and heated before the meat is placed on it.

When broiling by gas light the burners fully seven minutes before you place the meat under them, that the heat may be sufficient to sear the outer surface at once; otherwise the meat is likely to become tough and dry.

❧ STEWING

Use the less desirable parts of meat for stewing and allow plenty of time for cooking. Toughness is the almost inevitable consequence of hurried cooking. Stewing draws some of the juices out into the gravy. Stew meat by itself or add various vegetables; stews can be enriched by frying both meat and vegetables in a little fat before adding water or stock, thereby improving color and flavor. It is a decided advantage, when possible, to prepare and refrigerate a stew the day before it is to be served, as the cold fat can be removed from the gravy more easily. Stews made from meat that has been cooked previously require more seasoning and flavoring with sauces and other condiments than those in which fresh meat is used.

A stew is better and more savory if, before serving, the gravy is browned, seasoned, and thickened before the meat is added.

❧ FRYING

Frying is one of the most useful methods of cooking, especially to recook or reheat such small combinations as rissoles, croquettes, and small leftover dishes, which need little more than heating through and browning to give them an attractive appearance. Because frying is one of the least understood methods of cooking, as well as one of the most poorly performed, it has become discredited.

The difference between frying and sautéing should be clearly understood. The former requires sufficient fat in which to completely immerse the food to be fried; the latter requires only a little fat in the pan, but despite the seeming extravagance of "plenty of fat" the former is, for most foods, the better method of preparation and produces more digestible food.

The very best medium for frying is olive oil, but because the price is prohibitive for most people, vegetable oils are most commonly used. They are most pleasing to all and are free from cholesterol. Some people use lard, but others consider it to be unhealthy.

Use cast steel or aluminum pans because they retain the steady temperature required for frying; they should be fairly deep and have straight sides. A frying basket made of mesh wire is most convenient when you do a lot of frying. The advantage of the basket is that several pieces can be lowered into and raised from the cooking oil at one time, lessening the risk of breaking the food on lifting it from the oil. You must use a wire dipper or spoon if you do not have a basket.

The temperature of frying oil is very important. Some cooks use a thermometer to test oil to determine when it has reached the proper temperature for the particular food to be fried.

Cooking Methods for Fish

❧ SAUTÉING

Clean the fish thoroughly, wipe dry, and dip in either flour, egg and bread crumbs, or egg and cornmeal, and sauté in a shallow frying pan, putting only a small amount of fat in the pan. Cook until one side of the fish is brown, turn, and brown the other side. You may season fish either before or after cooking. Use lard, butter, drippings, vegetable oil, or bacon fat.

❧ FRYING

Clean the fish and wipe perfectly dry; then dip in beaten egg and bread crumbs or cornmeal (crumbs are preferable), patting them on well so that no loose ones fall off and burn in the fat; then plunge the fish, a few pieces at a time, into the fat, which must be very hot and in sufficient quantity to cover the fish completely. Cook until golden brown and drain well on paper towels before serving.

❧ BROILING

More oily fish, such as bluefish, salmon, herring, and mackerel, are best for broiling, though other kinds can be cooked this way.

Wipe the fish well, season with salt and pepper, and place between the wires of a well-greased broiler. Broil the flesh side first, then the skin side, turning once during the cooking process.

Drier varieties that are broiled must be well seasoned after cooking, with butter spread and lemon juice sprinkled over them just before serving.

❧ BOILING

Choose a small, compact fish or a firm slice of a large one. Cod, haddock, halibut, mackerel, and salmon are best for boiling.

Wash thoroughly and wrap in cheesecloth, tying the ends of the cloth loosely. Use a regulation fish kettle with a drainer or place a plate in a pan and lay the fish on it. This prevents the possibility of the cloth sticking to the bottom of the pan and makes it easier to remove the cooked fish. A tablespoon of vinegar added to the water keeps the fish a good color and its flesh firm.

The water should be quite hot, but not boiling, when you put the fish in. If you plunge it into actively boiling water its skin is likely to crack. As a further precaution, keep the water to a simmer during the cooking time. Allow an average time of about 6 minutes to the pound, unless the fish is very thick, when it should be cooked for 10 minutes per pound. When boiling small fish whole, leave the heads on, but remove the eyes.

❧ BAKING

Wash the fish well. The black skin on the inside of haddock, small cod, or any small whole fish can be removed by rubbing it briskly with a cloth or small brush dipped in salt. Dry the fish and, if it is to be stuffed, prepare the stuffing by the rule given in the recipe for Stuffed Walleyed Pike; place the dressing in the fish and sew up the opening with white thread. Dredge with flour. Lay the fish either flat or fastened with thread or skewers in the form of the letter *S* in a well-greased baking pan, preferably one kept for the purpose, and put a little dripping or bacon fat over top. If the oven is very hot, cover the fish with greased paper during the first part of baking to prevent it from becoming too brown, and baste frequently to prevent dryness.

CORNING

Scale, clean, and wash the fish carefully. Fillet the fish and sprinkle it generously on both sides with salt. Cover and let stand 1 hour; then wash off and pat dry with paper towels.

Make a small hole in the tail end of the fillets and insert a strong thread or string through the hole; hang in sunlight or a dry place with adequate ventilation. Allow the fillets to dry for about 2 or 3 days or until they are no longer moist. Indians and Eskimos preserved fish this way for centuries.

Cooking Corned Fish Before cooking corned fish, soak them in fresh water and let stand overnight in the refrigerator. Remove the fish and pat dry with paper towels. The fish may now be cooked.

Pan-Frying Corned Fish Heat oil, ¼ inch deep, in a heavy frying pan and fry for 5 to 10 minutes on each side, turning only once. Fillets are done when they flake easily when pricked with a fork. Sprinkle with pepper and garnish with lemon slices.

Broiled Corned Fish Wipe fish well, and place on a broiler pan; broil until they are lightly browned on both sides and flake easily. Sprinkle with pepper and dot with butter and fresh lemon juice before serving.

Smoking and Drying Techniques

✒ SMOKING FISH

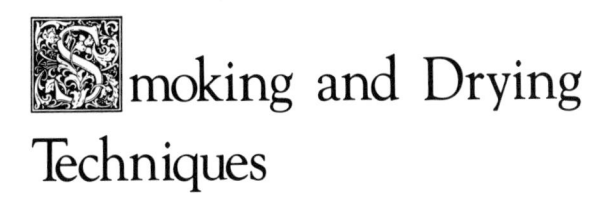

Smoking fish at one time was one of the few ways for early Americans to preserve fish. Today we have many methods, but some people still prefer the smoking method just for the flavor.

There are two methods used for smoking fish: the cold method, which takes about 5 days to complete, and the hot method, which takes only about 2 to 3 hours. The cold method preserves the fish almost indefinitely; the hot method preserves the fish for no longer than 2 weeks.

There are many ways to make your own smoker. The most popular requires a new, large metal garbage can with a lid, a piece of ½-inch mesh wire screen large enough to fit into the top of the can, two ¼-inch metal rods long enough to fit across the top of the can with about a ½ inch left over on each end, 1 foot of electrical conduit, a small singular-coiled hot plate, and a cast-iron skillet.

First, cut a 3-inch circular hole in the center of the garbage can lid. (A board is placed over this hole to regulate the draft.)

Drill four ¼-inch holes 6 inches below the top of the can; these holes are for the support rods that hold the mesh wire screen in place. Cut the mesh wire screen to fit on top of the rods.

Next, drill a ½-inch hole near the bottom of the can and insert the conduit. Set the hot plate in the bottom of the can and run the A.C. cord through the conduit. Place the skillet on the hot plate and fill it with green hickory chips, sweet wood sawdust, or other wood chips to provide the proper amount of smoke without flames. Choice of wood is a matter of personal taste. For a rich quality, the wood of any fruit tree will do, particularly apple or cherry. Other excellent woods for the purpose are maple, alder, birch, beech, and willow. Don't use wood from coniferous trees.

The main rule to remember when using a smoker is that you are smoking the fish, not cooking it.

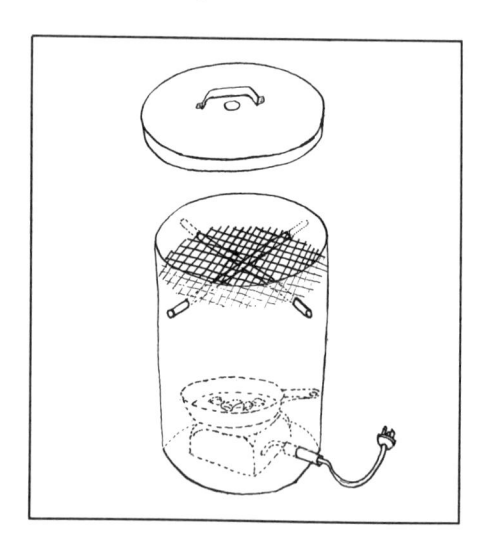

Preparing Fish for the Smoker

For 1 quart of brine:
- 1 quart water
- 2 tablespoons salt
- 4 tablespoons sugar
- ½ teaspoon tarragon
- ½ teaspoon cumin
- ½ teaspoon thyme

Clean the fish thoroughly and split them in half. Large fish may be filleted. Place the fish in a large stainless-steel or porcelain bowl; add brine to cover. Soak fish 2 to 3 hours for the hot method and overnight for the cold. The brine hardens the fish and also flavors it. After soaking, wash fish thoroughly with fresh water, then dry off before smoking.

Smoking Instructions

Place the fish on the mesh wire in the smoker, being careful that pieces do not touch each other. Plug in the hot plate and smoke 2 to 3 hours, with the lid on the can.

The fish is done when it feels firm. Take care not to oversmoke or the fish will become very hard.

≰ SMOKING MEAT

Smoked Wild Turkey

   1 wild turkey
   Seasoned salt
   Butter or margarine

Rinse the turkey inside and out, pat dry, and rub with seasoned salt. Fasten the neck skin to the back with skewers. Tie the wings to the body or tuck them in back of the bird. Leave the legs untied.

Prepare a charcoal fire in a smoker and let it burn for 15 minutes; add hickory wood chips to the fire. Place water pan in the smoker and fill with water.

Place the bird, breast side up, on the grill; brush with melted butter and cover with the lid. Allow the turkey to smoke 3½ to 4 hours (do not open the smoker during that time).

Smoked Goose

    1 goose, 6 to 8 pounds, cut up
    Salt
    1 teaspoon saltpeter
    ⅔ cup salt
    1 tablespoon sugar
    1 teaspoon garlic, minced

Skin the neck and reserve the whole skin. Chop the meat from the neck, wings, and back very fine. Stuff the chopped meat into the neck skin and tie both ends with heavy string; rub the neck, legs, and breast with salt. Mix the saltpeter, salt, sugar, and garlic and rub over the meat. Place in crock for 1 week. Remove and wrap each piece with cheesecloth, place in smoker, and smoke for 2 to 3 hours.

Smoked Quail

    12 to 16 quail
    Seasoned salt
    Butter or margarine

Wash quail inside and out, then wipe dry; rub with salt and butter. Prepare a charcoal fire in a smoker. Allow the fire to burn for about 15 minutes, then add some hickory wood chips. Add some water to the pan in the smoker. Place the quail on the grill and close the lid. Allow the quail to smoke for 1½ to 2½ hours.
    Serve quail immediately. Allow 2 birds per person.
    Quail may be reheated later if desired. To reheat, place quail slices in a shallow pan and sprinkle with water. Cover pan tightly, and bake at 425 degrees for about 10 to 12 minutes or until thoroughly heated.

Smoked Ham

½ cup saltpeter
2 cups fine salt
1 cup brown sugar
100 pounds ham
4 cups regular salt
3 tablespoons freshly ground black pepper
2 tablespoons red pepper

Combine saltpeter, fine salt, and sugar; mix well. Rub this mixture over ham and let stand for 24 hours. Then combine the regular salt and black pepper, rub over the ham, and let stand for 5 days. Rub on salt and pepper mixture again and let stand for 30 days. Brush off excess salt and smoke the ham with hickory wood chips for 10 days. After this, rub the meat with red pepper, wrap it in brown bags, and then in muslin bags. Hang hams hock down. Hams prepared this way will keep almost indefinitely.

Smoked Wild Boar Sausage

9 pounds lean boar meat
1 pound fat boar meat
4 tablespoons salt
½ teaspoon ginger
1 teaspoon sage
1 tablespoon black pepper
1 tablespoon red pepper

Cut wild boar meat into small pieces and add seasonings. Put mixture through sausage grinder twice. Stuff into sausage skins (skins may be purchased from your butcher), and smoke continuously for 4 days.

The best woods for smoking are hickory, apple, and sassafras.

DRYING MEAT

    20 pounds fresh meat
    2 cups salt
    1 teaspoon saltpeter
    ½ cup brown sugar

Place meat in a large crock. Combine salt, saltpeter, and brown sugar; mix well, then divide into 3 equal portions. Rub meat with 1 portion thoroughly; let stand for 1 day. Repeat this procedure the second day and the third. Let meat stand in crock for 1 week or more, then hang in warm area until meat stops dripping. Wrap with brown bags, then muslin bags, and hang in a cool place.

PART TWO

RECIPES

WILD GAME

Venison

Many people consider venison to be as delicious as beef, but only when it is properly handled and prepared. Venison is preferred not only for its flavor but because it is low in cholesterol.

Venison, much the same as beef, can be prepared in many different ways, but be careful not to overcook it.

Elk, moose, caribou, and antelope may be substituted for venison in these recipes.

Roast Saddle of Venison

6 pounds saddle of venison, larded
Fat
1 tablespoon salt
¼ teaspoon freshly ground black pepper
¼ teaspoon cayenne

Wipe saddle of venison with a damp cloth and rub with fat, then sprinkle with salt, pepper, and cayenne.

Bake in preheated oven at 450 degrees for 30 minutes; then reduce heat to 300 degrees and roast for 2 hours.

Serve sliced with your favorite sauce.

⚜ Tangy Roast Haunch of Venison

   3 cups pineapple-grapefruit juice
   1 teaspoon crushed rosemary
   ½ teaspoon oregano
   1 bay leaf
   ¼ cup parsley, finely chopped
   ½ cup wine vinegar
   ¼ cup green onion, chopped
   1 clove garlic, quartered
   1 teaspoon salt
   1 6-pound haunch venison, bone in
   2 tablespoons butter or margarine
   2 tablespoons all-purpose flour
   1 beef bouillon cube

Mix juice, rosemary, oregano, bay leaf, parsley, vinegar, onion, garlic, and salt. Place venison in deep container; pour juice mixture over venison. Refrigerate for 6 to 8 hours or overnight, turning venison twice. Remove venison from marinade; place in shallow roasting pan. Bake in preheated oven at 325 degrees for 3 hours. Remove venison from roasting pan; place on platter. In a separate pan, melt butter; stir in flour. Add bouillon cube and 2 cups marinade; bring to a boil, stirring constantly. Cook until sauce attains desired consistency. Slice venison; serve with hot sauce.

Buttered peas or string beans go well with this meal.

⚜ Apple Cider Venison Roast

   ½ teaspoon salt
   ¼ teaspoon freshly ground black pepper
   1 tablespoon dry mustard

3 tablespoons flour
½ cup apple cider
1 4-pound venison rump roast
1 cup currant jelly

Combine salt, pepper, mustard, and flour; blend in apple cider. Place venison roast on heavy-duty aluminum foil in a roasting pan. Pour cider mixture over top of roast. Close foil around roast securely. Bake in preheated oven at 300 degrees for 2 hours and 30 minutes. Remove roast from oven, open foil, and spread jelly over top of roast. Seal foil and return to the oven for 1 hour longer, basting with pan juices every 15 minutes.
Serve with baked potato, green salad, and freshly baked bread.

Apple Valley Venison Roast

6 thick slices salt pork, rinsed
5 pounds venison roast
½ teaspoon salt
¼ teaspoon freshly ground black pepper
3 tablespoons fresh lemon juice
½ cup dry white wine
2 tablespoons Worcestershire sauce
1 medium-sized onion, finely chopped

Rinse salt pork to wash off excess salt. Line roasting pan with salt pork and place venison roast in pan. Add all other ingredients and fill pan halfway with water. Bake in preheated oven at 325 degrees for about 3 hours or until tender. Baste several times while roasting, adding water when necessary. Slice servings across grain.
Nice with green beans, sweet potatoes, and coleslaw.

Venison Pot Roast

- 3 pounds venison rump roast, boneless
- All-purpose flour
- 2 tablespoons shortening, melted
- 2 cloves garlic, minced
- Salt and pepper
- ½ cup chopped onion
- ¾ cup water
- ¼ cup brown sugar
- ¼ cup dry red wine
- ¼ cup fresh lemon juice
- ½ teaspoon dry mustard
- ½ teaspoon paprika
- 2 bay leaves, crumbled

Dredge roast in flour; brown on all sides in shortening in a large skillet. Sprinkle garlic, salt, pepper, and onion over venison roast. Add water and bring to boil; reduce heat, cover, and simmer for 2 hours. Combine remaining ingredients and pour over venison roast. Cover and simmer for 1 hour or until roast is tender.

Serve with tender-crisp brussels sprouts mixed with peas and baked potato wedges.

Herbed Venison and Mushrooms

- 3 tablespoons butter
- 1 pound fresh mushrooms, sliced
- 3 medium onions, finely chopped
- ⅓ cup all-purpose flour
- 2 teaspoons salt
- ¼ teaspoon paprika
- ¾ teaspoon freshly ground black pepper

    2 pounds ¼-inch-thick venison steak
    ⅓ cup butter
    2 cloves garlic, crushed
      Pinch rosemary leaves
  1 ⅓ cups beef stock

Melt butter in a skillet; add mushrooms and onions and sauté until tender. Place mushrooms and onions in a 2-quart shallow casserole and set aside. Combine flour, salt, paprika, and pepper; dredge venison in flour mixture. Melt butter in skillet, add venison, and brown well. Place venison over onions and mushrooms in casserole. Top with garlic and rosemary. Pour beef stock over top. Loosen browned particles from skillet and add to casserole. Cover and bake at 350 degrees for 45 minutes. Serve sauce in gravy boat.

Nice with mashed potatoes. Garnish serving platter with fresh dill or watercress.

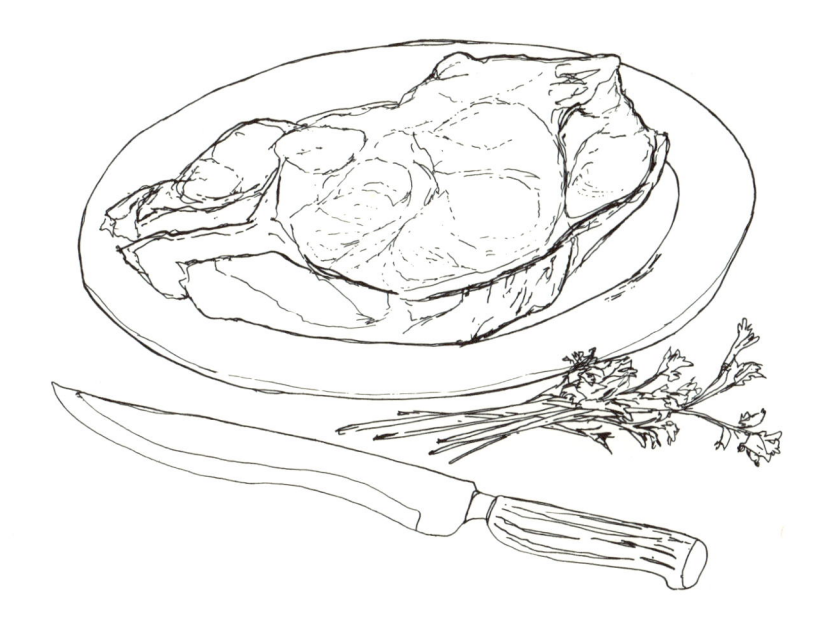

Venison Cutlet Casserole

    Salt and pepper
8 ¼-inch-thick venison cutlets, cut 5 by 2 inches
2 tablespoons prepared mustard
    Flour for dredging
1 medium onion, thinly sliced
¼ cup vegetable oil
2 tablespoons all-purpose flour
1½ cups tomato sauce
1 pound fresh mushrooms, sliced

Salt and pepper cutlets on both sides; coat with mustard, then dredge with flour. Set cutlets aside. Sauté onion in oil until browned; place in a greased 1-quart shallow casserole. Add 2 or 3 cutlets to skillet and cook over medium heat until brown on both sides, turning once. Place in casserole; repeat procedure until all cutlets are cooked. Stir all-purpose flour into pan drippings; cook, stirring constantly, until lightly browned. Gradually add tomato sauce; cook over medium heat, stirring constantly, until thickened. Pour over cutlets; add mushrooms. Cover and bake at 350 degrees for 1 hour.

    Serve sauce over hot cooked rice or mashed potatoes.

Venison Cutlet with Apple

4 apples
    Powdered sugar
½ cup port wine
    Butter or margarine
6 ½-inch-thick venison cutlets, cut 5 by 2 inches
    Salt
    Freshly ground black pepper
12 candied cherries

Wipe, core, and cut apples in ¼-inch slices. Sprinkle with powdered sugar, add wine, cover, and let stand 30 minutes. Drain (reserving wine) and sauté in butter. Sprinkle cutlets with salt and pepper, and cook for 3 or 4 minutes in lightly greased pan. Remove from pan. Melt 3 tablespoons butter in pan; add wine drained from apples. Reheat cutlets in sauce and serve with apples. Garnish with cherries.

BROILED VENISON WITH CORBIN STEAK SAUCE

Corbin Steak Sauce

- 2 tablespoons butter or margarine
- ½ cup dry white wine
- ¼ teaspoon garlic powder
- 1 tablespoon Worcestershire sauce
- 1 teaspoon paprika
- ½ teaspoon dry mustard
- 2 drops Tabasco sauce
- 1 teaspoon fresh lemon juice
- ½ teaspoon salt
- ¼ teaspoon freshly ground black pepper

Venison Steaks

2½ pounds venison steaks

Melt butter in saucepan over low heat; stir in remaining ingredients and mix well. Bring sauce to a boil and remove from heat.

Place venison steaks on broiler pan, brush on sauce, and broil for 5 minutes; turn and brush sauce on other side. Broil for 5 minutes or to desired doneness. Use sauce generously.

Broiled Venison Steak with Garlic Sauce

3 tablespoons butter
1 teaspoon garlic powder
½ cup A-1 sauce
3 tablespoons Worcestershire sauce
2½ pounds venison steaks

Melt butter in saucepan over low heat; add garlic powder, A-1 sauce, and Worcestershire sauce; mix well. Bring to a boil, then remove from heat. Place steaks on broiler pan. Brush on sauce, then broil for 5 minutes; turn and brush sauce on other side. Broil for 5 minutes or to desired doneness. Use sauce generously.

Venison Steak with Wine Sauce

½-inch-thick venison steaks
Butter or margarine, 1 tablespoon per pound venison
Salt and pepper to taste
Currant jelly, 1 tablespoon per pound venison
Dry red wine, 1 cup per 4 pounds venison

Place venison in hot buttered skillet. Sauté over high heat on both sides, sealing in juices, then reduce heat to low and cook for 5 minutes on one side. Turn venison steak over. Mix butter, salt, pepper, jelly, and wine in a chafing dish. Heat until jelly melts. Pour wine sauce over steaks and cook for 5 minutes more. Serve wine sauce in separate dish or ladled over steaks.

Serve with asparagus spears and scalloped potatoes.

Venison Chops in Wine

    6 venison chops, 2½ to 3 pounds
    1 large clove garlic, crushed
       Salt and pepper to taste
    4 tablespoons butter or margarine
    2 tablespoons olive oil
    8 scallions, chopped
    1 tablespoon parsley, finely chopped
    2 tablespoons flour
1½ cups dry white wine
    1 teaspoon fresh lemon juice
       Hot cooked rice

Rub chops with garlic; season with salt and pepper. Heat 2 tablespoons butter and olive oil in large skillet; add chops. Brown on both sides; remove to baking dish. Add remaining 2 tablespoons butter to skillet; sauté scallions and parsley until soft. Stir in flour and blend well; add wine and lemon juice gradually. Cook, stirring constantly, until mixture begins to thicken. Pour over chops; cover. Bake at 350 degrees for 25 minutes. Remove cover; continue baking for 10 minutes longer.

When chops are tender, remove them from sauce. Place hot cooked rice on heated platter; arrange chops on top. Pour sauce over chops and rice.

Garnish with tomato wedges and serve with fresh spinach salad and hot rolls.

Country-Style Venison

- 2 pounds venison chuck roast, boneless, cut into 1½-inch cubes
- 2 tablespoons vegetable oil
- 2 cups water
- ½ cup dry red wine
- 1 scallion, minced
- 1 tablespoon salt
- ½ teaspoon freshly ground black pepper
- 6 small white onions
- 6 small whole carrots
- 3 medium potatoes, pared and cubed
- 1 medium kohlrabi, pared and cubed
- 4 stalks celery, cut into 2-inch-long strips
- 1 pound fresh mushrooms, whole
- Hot cooked rice
- Fresh parsley

Brown venison cubes on all sides in hot oil in a large, heavy skillet. Add water, wine, scallion, salt and pepper; bring to a boil. Reduce heat; cover and simmer 1½ hours. Add vegetables; cover and simmer 20 minutes or until tender. Serve over hot cooked rice. Garnish with parsley.

Bryant County Venison

  1 cup onion, chopped
  4 tablespoons vegetable oil
  3 pounds venison, cut into 1-inch cubes
  ¼ cup all-purpose flour
1¼ teaspoons salt
  ½ teaspoon thyme leaves, whole
  1 bay leaf
  ⅛ teaspoon freshly ground black pepper
  ½ cup beef bouillon
  1 cup dry red wine
  ½ pound fresh mushrooms, sliced
  2 tablespoons butter, melted

Sauté onion in hot oil until tender. Dredge venison in flour and brown in oil. Add salt, thyme, bay leaf, pepper, bouillon, and wine; cook at a simmer for one hour, stirring occasionally. If necessary, add more wine or bouillon. Sauté mushrooms in butter; add meat and simmer for about 30 minutes more or until meat is tender.

Serve with potatoes or over rice or noodles.

Venison Casserole Claret

    4 pounds venison, cubed
    7 tablespoons butter or margarine
    4 tablespoons brandy
    12 small white onions
    12 small whole carrots
    1 6-ounce can black olives, pitted
    ¼ cup flour
    2 tablespoons tomato paste
    ¾ cup claret wine
    2 cups beef broth
    1 bay leaf
    3 medium potatoes, pared and cubed
    1 medium kohlrabi, pared and cubed
    ⅓ cup capers
    ½ teaspoon salt
    1 pound fresh mushrooms, halved

Brown venison in 3 tablespoons of butter in a large skillet. Pour brandy over venison and ignite. When flame subsides, place venison in 3-quart casserole. Place onions, carrots, and olives in the skillet with remaining 4 tablespoons butter and sauté until tender. Stir in flour and tomato paste; add wine, broth, and bay leaf. Cook, stirring constantly, until mixture thickens. Boil for 5 minutes. Add remaining ingredients, except mushrooms. Pour into casserole with venison cubes. Cover and bake at 350 degrees for 1¼ hours or until venison and vegetables are tender. Remove bay leaf, add mushrooms, and bake for 5 minutes more.

Sunset Venison Stew

- 2 pounds venison, cubed
- 3 tablespoons butter or margarine
- 1 8-ounce can tomato sauce
- 1 tablespoon all-purpose flour
- 1 tablespoon onion, minced
- 1 cup dry red wine
- 2 cloves garlic, crushed
- 6 peppercorns, crushed
- ⅛ teaspoon thyme
- 3 carrots, 1-inch slices
- 2 medium potatoes, pared and cubed
- 1 sweet green pepper, 1-inch cubes
- ½ pound fresh mushrooms, quartered

Brown venison in butter in a large skillet. Add remaining ingredients, except mushrooms. Cook, stirring constantly, until mixture is well blended and thickened. Simmer for 5 minutes. Pour into 3-quart casserole. Cover and bake at 350 degrees for 1½ hours or until meat and vegetables are tender. Remove from oven, add mushrooms, and bake for 5 minutes more.

❧ Orange Venison Stew

    1 pound fresh mushrooms, halved
    4 tablespoons shallots, minced
    6 tablespoons butter or margarine
    1 cup dry white wine
    2 pounds venison, cubed
    ¼ cup flour for dredging
    3 tomatoes, quartered
    2 green peppers, 1-inch cubes
    2 large potatoes, pared and cubed
    8 small white onions
    1 teaspoon orange peel, grated
    2 tablespoons all-purpose flour
1½ cups beef broth
    1 bay leaf

Sauté mushrooms and shallots in 4 tablespoons of butter in a large skillet. Add wine; cook over high heat until reduced to half. Pour mixture into 3-quart casserole. Dredge venison lightly in flour and sauté in remaining 2 tablespoons butter. Add tomatoes, pepper, potatoes and onions; sauté for 5 minutes, stirring frequently. Add orange peel. Stir in flour. Add beef broth. Cook, stirring constantly, until mixture thickens. Boil for 1 minute. Stir mixture into casserole; add bay leaf. Cover; bake at 350 degrees for 1¼ hours or until meat and vegetables are tender. Remove bay leaf before serving.

❧ Barbecued Venison Kabobs

3 pounds 1½-inch-thick venison steak, cut into 1½-inch cubes
1 pound fresh mushroom caps
1 cup dry red wine
2 green bell peppers, cut into 1-inch pieces and parboiled

18 whole potatoes (egg size), parboiled
18 cherry tomatoes

Combine meat, mushrooms, and wine in a shallow dish. Cover and marinate for 2 to 3 hours in the refrigerator. Remove meat and mushrooms from marinade. Alternate vegetables and meat on skewers. Grill for 10 to 15 minutes over medium heat or until desired degree of doneness is reached.

Venison Meatballs and Wine Sauce

1½ pounds ground venison
¼ cup onion, chopped
¼ cup green pepper, chopped
⅓ cup tomato sauce
1 egg
1 teaspoon salt
⅛ teaspoon freshly ground black pepper
¾ cup bread crumbs
½ teaspoon garlic powder
2 tablespoons vegetable oil

Combine first nine ingredients; mix well. Shape mixture into meatballs. Place meatballs in vegetable oil in a large, heavy skillet and brown.

Wine Sauce

¼ cup dry red wine
1 cup tomato sauce
¾ cup tomato paste
¼ cup water
1½ teaspoons oregano leaves, crushed
¼ teaspoon salt

Combine all ingredients; mix well. Pour mixture over meatballs in skillet. Cover; simmer for about 30 minutes.

Uncle Herbert's Secret Venison Chili

- 2 pounds venison, ground
- ½ cup onion, chopped
- 2 tablespoons chili pods, diced
- 2 14½-ounce cans whole tomatoes, undrained and chopped
- 1 6-ounce can tomato paste
- 1 12-ounce can beer
- 1 cup beef stock
- 1 15-ounce can red kidney beans
- 2 cloves garlic, minced
- 2 teaspoons salt
- 1 teaspoon cumin, ground
- ¼ teaspoon freshly ground white pepper
- ¼ teaspoon cayenne
- ¼ teaspoon paprika
- 2 teaspoons chili powder
- 1 ounce milk chocolate

Brown venison in large skillet; drain off any liquid that forms. Sauté onions until tender in separate saucepan; add to browned venison. Add all other ingredients and simmer for 2 hours.

Serve with freshly baked bread and beer.

Pine Mountain Venison Chili and Beans

- 2½ pounds venison, ground
- ½ cup beef suet, chopped
- 6 cups water
- 2 bay leaves
- 6 cloves garlic, crushed
- 4 teaspoons chili powder

    2 teaspoons salt
    2 teaspoons ground cumin
    1 teaspoon oregano leaves
    2 tablespoons brown sugar
    ½ teaspoon Tabasco sauce
    1 15-ounce can tomato sauce
    ½ cup onion, chopped
    2½ cups kidney beans, cooked

Combine venison and suet in large skillet and cook until browned, stirring to crumble. Add water and bay leaves; cover and simmer over low heat for 1½ hours. Add next 9 ingredients; simmer for 30 minutes. Stir in beans; simmer an additional 15 or 20 minutes. Remove bay leaves before serving.

Grandma's Venisonburgers

    1½ pounds venison, ground
    1½ cups corn flakes cereal
    1 large onion, finely chopped
    1 teaspoon fresh parsley, chopped
    2 tablespoons black walnuts, chopped
    1 small apple, peeled and finely chopped
    1 stalk celery, finely chopped
    1 tomato, finely chopped
    1½ teaspoons freshly ground black pepper
    1 teaspoon salt
    2 tablespoons butter or margarine, melted

Combine all ingredients, except butter, and mix well. Shape into patties and brush with butter. Broil for about 5 minutes on each side, depending on desired degree of doneness.

❦ Venison Meatloaf

  1½ pounds venison, ground
  1½ cups bread crumbs
    1 cup milk
    1 egg, beaten
    1 teaspoon salt
    ¼ teaspoon freshly ground black pepper
    ¼ teaspoon garlic powder
    ¼ cup onion, minced
    1 tablespoon Worcestershire sauce
    ¼ cup tomato catsup (for top of loaf)

Mix all ingredients, except catsup, thoroughly in large bowl. Shape into loaf pan and bake in preheated oven at 350 degrees for about 1 hour. Remove from oven and spread catsup over top; return to oven and bake for ½ hour longer.

Serve green beans, mashed potatoes, gravy, and hot rolls with this dish.

❦ Venison Sausage

  10 pounds ground venison
    ¼ pound salt
    1 teaspoon sugar
    ½ teaspoon ginger
    1 tablespoon freshly ground black pepper
    1 teaspoon sage
    1 teaspoon liquid smoke

Mix all ingredients well in a large bowl and divide into 10 equal portions. Roll each portion in aluminum foil, making elongated rolls, then store them in a freezer.

The sausage rolls may be sliced and fried in a skillet or placed whole on a broiler pan; first make 4 or 5 small punctures in rolls to allow the juices to drain. Bake at 350 degrees for 1½ hours.

VENISON TONGUE

- 1 venison tongue, about 2 pounds
- 1 small onion, chopped
- 4 cloves, whole
- 2 small bay leaves
- 1 tablespoon salt
- ½ teaspoon red pepper
- 1 ½-inch slice lemon

Clean tongue thoroughly, scrubbing and rinsing. Put in large pan and cover with boiling water. Add all ingredients, cover, and simmer slowly (do not boil) for 3 or 4 hours or until tender. Allow to cool slightly in stock. Drain and remove skin and fat. Serve hot with wine sauce or sliced cold with tangy sauce.

Serve with fluffy mashed potatoes, buttered baby beets, and a green salad.

Venison Tongue Wine Sauce

- 1½ tablespoons prepared mustard
- ⅓ cup dry white wine
- ½ cup sour cream
- 2 teaspoons butter or margarine, melted
- ⅛ teaspoon salt
- ½ teaspoon dried parsley flakes

Combine all ingredients in a small saucepan. Cook over low heat until sauce is warm, stirring constantly. Yields 1 cup.

Venison Tongue Tangy Sauce

- 1 teaspoon dry mustard
- ¾ cup mayonnaise
- ¼ cup dry white wine
- 1½ teaspoons fresh lime juice
- ⅛ teaspoon salt
- ⅛ teaspoon Tabasco sauce
- Dash freshly ground white pepper

Combine all ingredients in small bowl, mixing well. Yields a little over 1 cup.

Sautéed Venison Liver with Apple Slices

- 1 pound venison liver
- Salt
- Freshly ground black pepper
- 4 tablespoons butter or margarine
- ¼ cup onion, chopped
- ½ cup apple slices, peeled
- Brown sugar
- Cinnamon

Slice venison liver into ½-inch slices; sprinkle with salt and pepper. Melt 2 tablespoons butter in skillet, add chopped onion and venison liver slices, and sauté for about 5 minutes (overcooking toughens liver). Melt remaining butter and fry apples in a separate saucepan on low heat until tender and done. Serve liver topped with cooked apple slices sprinkled with brown sugar and cinnamon.

Garnish with crisp bacon strips and tomato wedges. Nice with freshly baked biscuits.

Bear

Bear Steak Rollups

    1 pound ½-inch thick round bear steak, boneless
    ½ cup fresh mushrooms, chopped
    ¼ cup bread crumbs
    1 medium tomato, peeled and finely chopped
    1 teaspoon orange rind, grated
    ½ teaspoon freshly ground black pepper
1¼ teaspoons salt
    ¼ cup all-purpose flour
    ¼ cup vegetable oil
    1 cup peas
    2 cups baby carrots, whole
    3 celery stalks, cut into 1½-inch pieces
    2 cups beef broth
    2 tablespoons water
    Hot cooked rice

Trim and pound steak to ¼-inch thickness and cut into 3½-by-4½-inch pieces. Combine mushrooms, bread crumbs, tomato, orange rind, ¼ teaspoon pepper, and 1 teaspoon salt. Place 2 tablespoons of mixture on each steak, spreading to within ½ inch of edge. Roll up each piece, securing with toothpicks. Combine flour, ¼ teaspoon salt, and ¼ teaspoon pepper. Dredge bear steak rollups in flour mixture, reserving excess mixture. Brown rollups in hot oil. Place in 2-quart casserole or baking dish; add peas, carrots, celery, and broth. Cover and bake at 375 degrees for 1 hour or until tender. Remove rollups from casserole, reserving drippings; remove toothpicks. Place rollups and vegetables on cooked rice. Combine reserved flour mixture and 2 tablespoons water in a small saucepan, blending until smooth. Gradually stir in drippings; cook over medium heat, stirring constantly, until thickened and bubbly. Serve gravy with rollups.

Bear Hot Pot

2 pounds bear steak, cubed
2 pounds potatoes
4 onions
Salt
Freshly ground black pepper
¼ teaspoon cayenne
All-purpose flour
Water or stock

Cut meat into serving-sized pieces. Peel potatoes and cut them into small, thick pieces; slice onions thinly. Mix salt, pepper, cayenne, and flour and roll each piece of meat in the mixture. Put a layer of potatoes in a deep dish or bowl (a wide-mouthed bean pot is a satisfactory dish), then a layer of meat, next sliced onions, repeating the process till the dish is filled, ending with potatoes for the top layer. Fill the dish with water or stock. Bake in a moderate oven for 3 hours, adding more water if necessary. Serve in the dish in which it was cooked.

Rolled Bear Steak Loaf

- 2 pounds ½-inch-thick round bear steak, boneless
- 1 teaspoon salt
- ¼ teaspoon freshly ground black pepper
- 1 small onion, finely chopped
- 1 tablespoon parsley, finely chopped
- 1 cup dry bread crumbs
- 1 pound pork sausage meat
- 2 tablespoons butter or margarine, melted
- 2 tablespoons flour

Trim off excess fat and pound bear steak with tenderizing mallet until tender; leave steak in one piece. Salt and pepper both sides. Cover entire top surface with onion, parsley, and bread crumbs. Then spread on pork sausage meat. Roll into a loaf and tie with a cord in several places to hold together. Brush outer surface with butter and sprinkle with flour. Bake at 350 degrees for 1 to 1½ hours.

Serve with cooked rice and freshly baked bread.

Bear Cubes in Wine Sauce

¼ cup vegetable oil
3 pounds bear roast, boneless, cut into 1-inch cubes
3 tablespoons all-purpose flour
1½ cups beef broth
5 shallots, chopped
1 bay leaf
⅛ teaspoon ground thyme
5 potatoes, cut into slices, cooked, and drained
1 cup onions, boiled
1 pound fresh mushrooms, sautéed in butter
2½ cups dry red wine

Heat oil in large skillet; brown bear cubes slowly on all sides. Place cubes in a 4-quart casserole; reserve pan drippings. Add flour to pan drippings; cook over low heat for 1 minute, stirring constantly. Gradually stir in broth; add shallots. Cook over medium heat, stirring constantly, until thickened. Pour over bear cubes, stir in bay leaf and thyme. Bake at 300 degrees for 2 hours or until meat is tender. Add potatoes, onions, mushrooms, and wine; bake for 15 minutes more or until vegetables are thoroughly heated.

Serve with noodles or wild rice and hot rolls.

Raccoon

❧ CUMBERLAND VALLEY COON

   2 teaspoons salt
  ½ teaspoon red pepper
   4 cloves garlic, crushed
   1 coon, whole, skinned and cleaned
  ½ cup butter or margarine
   1 onion, thinly sliced
   1 carrot, sliced
   1 turnip, sliced
   1 bay leaf
   1 sprig thyme
   1 sprig parsley
   3 cups hot water
1½ teaspoons salt
    Peppercorns
   4 tablespoons all-purpose flour

Place coon in large pot, cover with water, and add salt, pepper, and garlic. Parboil until meat is tender. Remove from heat and drain. Place coon in a deep baking pan with cover. Melt ¼ cup butter in a separate skillet; add onion, carrot, turnip, bay leaf, thyme, parsley, hot water, salt, and peppercorns; cook over medium heat for 5 minutes. Pour mixture over coon. Cover tightly and bake in slow oven (250 degrees) for 3 hours, uncovering for the last half hour. Remove from pan to hot platter. Melt remaining butter in separate skillet, add flour, and stir until well browned; then pour on the strained liquid slowly (there should be 1½ cups). Cook until desired thickness is reached. Serve with coon. Coon should be carved into sections for individual servings.

Marinated Coon

- 1½ cups beer
- ⅔ cup catsup
- ½ cup onion, chopped
- ¼ cup sugar
- 3 tablespoons fresh lemon juice
- 2 tablespoons Worcestershire sauce
- 1 teaspoon salt
- 1 teaspoon paprika
- ½ teaspoon chili powder
- ⅛ teaspoon freshly ground black pepper
- 1½ to 2 pounds coon, cut up

Combine beer, catsup, onion, sugar, lemon juice, Worcestershire sauce, salt, paprika, chili powder, and pepper in a large saucepan; simmer, uncovered, for 15 minutes. Cool. Place coon in plastic bag; set in a shallow dish. Pour in beer marinade. Close bag. Let stand in refrigerator overnight. Remove coon from beer marinade. Place meat on unheated rack in broiler pan; broil 3 inches from heat for 10 to 15 minutes per side, brushing with marinade occasionally.

Serve with buttered peas and limas and celery slaw.

Possum

✹ Possum with Brandy and Wine Sauce

4 to 5 pounds possum, cut up
Salt
Red pepper
¼ cup brandy
1 cup dry red wine
½ teaspoon dried thyme
½ teaspoon dried marjoram
¼ teaspoon allspice
3 tablespoons buter or margarine
3 tablespoons vegetable oil
1 cup onion, chopped
2 cloves garlic, finely minced
1 pound fresh mushrooms, thinly sliced
¾ cup rich beef stock

Rinse possum pieces and dry thoroughly with paper towels. Sprinkle generously with salt and red pepper. Combine next 5 ingredients for the marinade in a large bowl; add possum pieces. Cover the bowl and refrigerate for at least 5 hours, turning the pieces of possum several times during marination.

Remove possum from the marinade and let excess liquid drain

back into bowl. Place possum on a platter and set aside.

Melt butter in a heavy skillet over medium heat, then add vegetable oil and mix well. When the oil is quite hot, add possum pieces and brown well on all sides (about 15 to 20 minutes). Add the remaining ingredients and ½ cup strained marinade. Cook over medium heat until liquid begins to bubble. Reduce heat to low, cover, and cook until possum is tender (about 1½ hours). Serve from the skillet and spoon sauce over each portion.

⚶ Southern Baked Possum

- 2 teaspoons salt
- ½ teaspoon red pepper
- 4 cloves garlic, crushed
- 1 possum, whole, cleaned and dressed
- ½ cup port wine
- ½ cup melted butter or margarine
- 1 onion, thinly sliced
- ¼ teaspoon celery salt
- 2 sprigs thyme
- 1 cup chicken stock
- Pinch cayenne

Place possum in large pot; cover with water, add salt, red pepper, and garlic; parboil until meat is tender. Drain and place in deep baking pan with cover. Add all other ingredients, cover, and bake in preheated oven at 250 degrees for 3 hours, basting occasionally in own juices. Add water if needed. Uncover and bake for 30 minutes longer. Possum should be carved into sections for individual servings.

Serve with baked quartered Irish potatoes or candied yams, green beans, mixed green salad, and crisp Italian bread.

Rabbit

❧ Kentucky Rabbit

- 3 pounds rabbit, cut up
- Salt
- Freshly ground black pepper
- Flour for dredging
- ¼ pound butter or margarine
- ¼ cup dry white wine
- 1 cup fresh mushrooms, sliced
- 1 cup milk
- 1 celery stalk, cut into ½-inch sections
- ¼ cup onion, finely chopped
- 4 tablespoons all-purpose flour
- 1 cup water

Place rabbit in bowl; add 1½ tablespoons salt and cover with cold water; let stand for 3 hours. Drain, wipe, sprinkle with salt and pepper, and roll in flour. Melt butter in deep skillet over medium heat. Put rabbit in skillet and fry for 20 to 30 minutes, turning occasionally. Add remaining ingredients and cook slowly for 1 hour, turning rabbit frequently.

Garnish with parsley. Serve with vegetables and gravy over hot cooked rice.

Pan-Fried Rabbit with Country Colonel Gravy

⅓ cup all-purpose flour
1½ teaspoons salt
⅛ teaspoon freshly ground black pepper
2½ to 3 pounds rabbit, cut up
Vegetable oil

Combine flour, salt, and pepper in a plastic bag. Add rabbit pieces, two at a time; shake well to coat.

Heat ½-inch-deep vegetable oil to 375 degrees in a large skillet. Add rabbit pieces. Fry, uncovered, on one side for about 5 minutes or until browned. Turn pieces. Cover skillet; cook for another 5 minutes or until second side is browned. Uncover; turn again. Cook for 5 minutes or until pieces are crispy.

Serve with gravy and hot biscuits.

Country Colonel Gravy

¼ cup drippings
⅓ cup all-purpose flour
¾ cup milk
¾ cup water
Salt and pepper to taste

Prepare gravy in skillet in which the rabbit was fried. Drain all but ¼ cup drippings from skillet. Cook over medium heat; add flour, stirring until it turns a rich dark brown. Combine milk and water and pour into skillet; stir constantly until the gravy thickens and bubbles. Season with salt and pepper.

Rabbit with Mushroom Sauce

¼ teaspoon salt
¼ teaspoon freshly ground black pepper
¼ teaspoon paprika

¼ teaspoon onion salt
½ cup all-purpose flour
2½ to 3 pounds rabbit, cut up
4 tablespoons butter or margarine
2 cans cream of chicken soup
1 cup sour cream
1 cup fresh mushrooms, sliced

Combine salt, pepper, paprika, onion salt, and flour; dredge cut-up rabbit in mixture. Melt butter in skillet and brown pieces of rabbit on both sides. Remove rabbit to casserole. Combine soup and sour cream; spoon over rabbit. Cover; bake in preheated oven at 350 degrees for 1 hour or until tender. Remove rabbit from oven, add mushrooms, and return to oven for 15 minutes longer.

Serve with hot cooked rice or mashed potatoes, baked parsnips, and lima beans.

Lemon-Broiled Rabbit

3 to 4 pounds rabbit, cut up
Juice of 1 lemon
1½ teaspoons salt
1½ teaspoons freshly ground black pepper
1 teaspoon garlic, very finely minced
½ teaspoon ground rosemary
2 teaspoons fresh parsley, finely minced
1 stick butter or margarine, melted

Wash and dry rabbit pieces. Sprinkle rabbit with lemon juice. Combine salt, pepper, garlic, rosemary, and parsley, then sprinkle both sides with mixture.

Place rabbit skin side down on a hot broiling rack about 8 inches from the heat. Pour butter over rabbit and broil for 20 minutes on each side.

Serve with collards, fried okra, and shuck beans.

Rabbit in Wine Sauce

- 4 tablespoons butter or margarine
- 2 pounds rabbit, cut up
- ½ cup white wine
- ½ teaspoon salt
- ¼ teaspoon freshly ground black pepper
- ¼ teaspoon paprika
- 1 cup fresh mushroom caps
- 1 can cream of mushroom soup
- ½ cup toasted almonds, halved

Melt butter in skillet; brown rabbit on both sides. Place rabbit in casserole. Combine wine, salt, pepper, paprika, mushrooms, and soup; pour over rabbit. Bake in preheated oven at 350 degrees for 1 hour or until meat is tender. Garnish with almonds.

Serve over noodles.

Sage Rabbit

- 1 cup all-purpose flour
- ¾ cup grated Parmesan cheese
- 1 teaspoon sage
- ½ teaspoon salt
- ¼ teaspoon freshly ground black pepper
- ⅓ cup milk
- 1 egg
- 2½ to 3 pounds rabbit, cut up
- ¼ cup butter or margarine, melted

Combine flour, cheese, sage, salt, and pepper. Combine milk and egg in a separate bowl. Coat rabbit in flour mixture; then dip in milk mixture and once again in flour mixture. Place rabbit pieces in large, shallow baking pan. Drizzle butter over rabbit and bake in preheated oven at 400 degrees for 45 minutes or until meat is tender and crust is golden brown.

Serve with home-fried potatoes, pickled beets, tangy coleslaw, and freshly baked corn bread.

Hot Spiced Rabbit

½ cup white wine
2 tablespoons fresh lemon juice
¼ teaspoon garlic powder
½ teaspoon nutmeg
⅛ teaspoon ginger
4 pounds rabbit, cut up
9 hard-boiled eggs, chopped
2 cans cream of celery coup
1 can chicken soup
1½ cups mayonnaise
¼ teaspoon rosemary
¼ teaspoon basil
½ cup onions, chopped
Salt and pepper to taste
1 cup walnuts, chopped

Combine wine, lemon juice, garlic powder, nutmeg, and ginger. Place rabbit in baking pan; pour mixture over top. Cover and bake in preheated oven at 350 degrees for 1 hour. Let rabbit cool, remove bones, and chop meat coarsely. Add remaining ingredients, except walnuts. Place in baking dish and bake at 350 degrees for 30 minutes. Garnish with chopped walnuts.

Serve over noodles or rice with freshly baked biscuits.

The Colonel's Favorite Rabbit Recipe

- ½ cup butter or margarine
- 1 cup milk
- 1 egg, lightly beaten
- 1 cup all-purpose flour
- ¼ cup walnuts, chopped
- ½ cup pecans, chopped
- 1 teaspoon paprika
- 1 teaspoon salt
- ¼ teaspoon freshly ground black pepper
- ¼ cup sunflower seeds, chopped
- 2½ to 3 pounds rabbit, cut up

Melt butter in a baking dish. Blend milk and egg in a shallow dish. Combine flour, walnuts, pecans, paprika, salt, pepper, and sunflower seeds in a separate dish. Dip rabbit in milk mixture; roll in flour mixture. Place rabbit in melted butter in baking dish. Bake at 350 degrees, uncovered, for 1 hour or until meat is tender.

Serve with coleslaw, mashed potatoes, gravy, and freshly baked bread.

Oven-Fried Sesame Rabbit

- 1 egg, well beaten
- ⅓ cup milk
- ¾ cup all-purpose flour
- 2 teaspoons paprika
- ⅛ teaspoon freshly ground white pepper
- 1 teaspoon baking powder
- ½ cup pecans, finely chopped
- 2 tablespoons sesame seeds
- 1 teaspoon salt
- ½ cup butter or margarine, melted
- 2½ to 3 pounds rabbit, cut up

Combine egg and milk and mix well. Combine flour, paprika, pepper, baking powder, pecans, sesame seeds, and salt in a separate bowl. Pour butter into 15-by-10-by-1-inch pan and spread evenly. Dip rabbit in egg mixture, then dredge in flour mixture and place in pan. Bake in preheated oven at 325 degrees for 40 minutes; turn rabbit and bake for another 40 minutes or until meat is tender.

Serve with baked sweet potatoes or whole kernel corn and fresh turnip greens.

Coriander Rabbit and Wild Rice

- 1 6-ounce package wild rice mix
- ¼ cup butter or margarine
- ⅓ cup onion, chopped
- ¼ cup fresh coriander, chopped
- 1 egg, beaten lightly
- 1 teaspoon salt
  Dash freshly ground black pepper
- 3 pounds rabbit, cut up
- ⅓ cup all-purpose flour
- 1 cup rich chicken broth
- 1 cup half-and-half
- 1 teaspoon parsley, finely chopped

Prepare rice according to package directions. Melt butter in a heavy saucepan; add onion and coriander and sauté until onion is transparent. Blend together egg, salt, and pepper in a shallow dish. Dip rabbit in mixture; then place in skillet and sauté until meat is tender. Remove rabbit from skillet. Add flour to drippings and brown over medium heat, stirring constantly. Gradually add broth and half-and-half; cook, stirring constantly, until thickened. Stir in rice and parsley. Place rabbit in greased 2-quart casserole and cover with saucepan mixture. Bake in preheated oven at 425 degrees for 30 minutes or until bubbly.

Crusty Oven-Fried Rabbit

1 cup bread crumbs
1 teaspoon salt
¼ cup Parmesan cheese, grated
¼ teaspoon garlic powder
¼ teaspoon freshly ground black pepper
2 tablespoons parsley, finely chopped
½ cup butter or margarine, melted
2 pounds rabbit, cut up

Combine bread crumbs, salt, cheese, garlic powder, pepper, and parsley. Dip rabbit in melted butter and dredge in bread crumb mixture. Place rabbit in pan and bake in preheated oven at 350 degrees for 1 hour or until meat is tender.

Serve with new potatoes steamed in butter, okra and tomatoes, and corn bread muffins.

Italian Rabbit with Almonds

Salt and pepper
2 pounds rabbit, cut up
2 eggs, beaten
1 cup Italian-style bread crumbs
2 cups mozzarella cheese, shredded
¾ cup blanched almonds, chopped

Salt and pepper rabbit lightly. Dip each piece in egg, then coat with bread crumbs. Place pieces in a buttered baking pan. Bake in preheated oven at 350 degrees for 1 hour or until tender. Sprinkle cheese and almonds over rabbit. Return rabbit to oven and bake for 5 minutes longer or until cheese melts.

Serve with broccoli, brussels sprouts, and home-fried potatoes.

Rabbit and Cheese Casserole

- 4 cups rabbit, cooked and cubed
- 9 slices white bread, crusts removed
- 1 cup fresh mushrooms, sliced
- ¼ cup butter or margarine, melted
- 1 cup potatoes, sliced
- 3 slices mozzarella cheese
- 3 slices sharp process cheddar cheese
- 3 slices American cheese
- ½ cup mayonnaise
- 4 eggs, well beaten
- 2 cups milk
- 1 teaspoon salt
- 1 10¾-ounce can cream of celery soup
- 1 10¾-ounce can cream of mushroom soup
- 1 2-ounce jar chopped pimiento
- 2 cups buttered bread crumbs
- ½ cup cashew nuts, chopped

Place rabbit cubes in a buttered 13-by-9-by-2-inch baking dish lined with bread slices. Sauté mushrooms in butter and spoon over rabbit. Top with potatoes and cheese. Combine mayonnaise, eggs, milk, and salt; beat well. Pour mixture over cheese. Combine soups and pimiento, mixing well; spoon over casserole. Bake, uncovered, at 350 degrees for 30 minutes. Remove from oven; top with bread crumbs and nuts. Return to oven and bake for another 15 to 20 minutes.

Lemon-Baked Rabbit

    1 tablespoon butter or margarine
    2 tablespoons onion, finely chopped
    ½ teaspoon garlic, minced
    2 cups celery, thinly sliced
    ½ cup cashew nuts, halved
    2 cups cooked leftover rabbit meat, diced
    ½ cup heavy cream
    Juice of 1 lemon
    ½ teaspoon salt
    ¼ teaspoon freshly ground black pepper
    2 cups dry bread crumbs
    ½ cup mild cheddar cheese

Melt butter over medium heat in a skillet and add onion, garlic, celery, and cashews; sauté until onion is clear. Stir in rabbit meat, cream, lemon juice, salt, and pepper; then set aside.

Combine bread crumbs and cheese. Place 1 cup of bread crumb and cheese mixture into a well-greased 8-inch-square baking dish. Spoon rabbit mixture over bread crumbs; top with remaining bread crumbs and cheese.

Bake at 450 degrees for 15 minutes or until hot and bubbly.

Brunswick Stew

- 2 squirrels, cut up
- 1 rabbit, cut up
- 1 mountain quail, cut up
- 5 quarts boiling water
- ½ pound sugar-cured bacon
- ½ cup onion, chopped
- ½ cup cabbage, shredded
- 4 cups tomatoes, chopped
- 1 cup frozen lima beans
- 1 cup frozen whole-kernel sweet corn
- 1 cup navy beans
- 1 cup celery, chopped
- 1 cup carrots, sliced into ½-inch rounds
- 1 cup noodles, uncooked
- 6 potatoes, peeled and cubed
- 1 tablespoon salt
- 1 teaspoon freshly ground black pepper
- ½ teaspoon allspice
- ¼ teaspoon thyme
- ½ teaspoon garlic, minced
- 1 tablespoon parsley, finely chopped
- 4 tablespoons butter or margarine, melted
- 4 tablespoons flour, browned

Place squirrels, rabbit, and quail into boiling water in a large kettle. Add bacon and simmer for two hours, removing foam as it forms on top. Add next 16 ingredients and bring to a boil, reduce heat, and simmer for 1 hour longer or until vegetables are tender.

Mix butter and flour; shape into small balls and drop into stew; boil for 10 minutes or until the balls are smooth and thickened.

This stew is great at picnics and barbecues.

Squirrel

❧ Mountain Fried Squirrel and Gravy

2 pounds squirrel, cut up (cut each squirrel into six pieces)
Milk
Flour
Salt
Pepper
Vegetable oil

Select young squirrels if possible or parboil old ones. Dip squirrel in milk and roll in flour seasoned with salt and pepper. Fry squirrel in hot vegetable oil until brown on both sides and meat is done. Remove squirrels from skillet and keep warm.

Gravy

3 tablespoons of oil squirrel was fried in
¼ stick butter or margarine
2 tablespoons flour
1 teaspoon chives, chopped
1 teaspoon parsley, chopped

½ cup chicken broth
½ cup light cream
Salt and pepper

To make a cup of squirrel gravy, pour off all but 3 tablespoons of cooking oil left in skillet. Add all ingredients and stir over low heat until hot and of desired consistency.

Serve with fried apples, wild rice or mashed potatoes, hot biscuits, and currant jelly.

Squirrel in Orange and Honey Sauce

1 package wild rice mix
2 pounds squirrel, cut up
Salt to taste
Butter or margarine
½ cup honey
½ cup frozen orange juice
1 tablespoon fresh lemon juice
1 cup dry white wine
4 slices bacon, halved
Orange slices

Prepare rice according to package directions. Sprinkle squirrel with salt. Melt butter in skillet and brown squirrel; remove from heat and place pieces in baking pan. Combine honey, orange juice, lemon juice, and wine. Pour mixture over squirrel; top with bacon slices. Bake in preheated oven at 350 degrees for 1 hour. Remove squirrel and bacon; arrange on warm platter. Drain off sauce and pour over squirrel and rice. Garnish with orange slices.

Curried Squirrel and Rice

4 pounds squirrel, cut up
Flour for dredging, seasoned with salt and pepper
Vegetable oil
2 onions, finely chopped
2 green peppers, chopped
1 clove garlic, minced
1 teaspoon salt
5 cups whole tomatoes
2 teaspoons curry powder
1 teaspoon sugar
1 teaspoon parsley, finely chopped
½ teaspoon thyme
Hot water
4 cups cooked rice
3 tablespoons currants or white raisins
½ cup toasted almonds, chopped

Dredge squirrel in flour seasoned with salt and pepper. Place enough vegetable oil in frying pan to measure ½ inch deep. Fry squirrel pieces until brown on all sides. Remove squirrel from pan and drain all but 3 tablespoons of oil. Add onions, peppers, and garlic to oil; sauté for 5 minutes over low heat, stirring constantly. Mix in salt, tomatoes, curry powder, sugar, parsley, and thyme. Place squirrel in large casserole; pour mixture over pieces, adding enough hot water to cover. Cover tightly and bake in preheated oven at 350 degrees for about 45 minutes or until meat is tender. Serve squirrel over rice. Garnish with currants and almonds.

Lemon-Fried Squirrel

    3 pounds squirrel, cut up
    ½ teaspoon salt
    ½ teaspoon freshly ground black pepper
    ¼ cup vegetable oil
    ⅓ cup fresh lemon juice
    ½ teaspoon sugar
    ¼ teaspoon paprika
    ¼ teaspoon prepared mustard
    ⅛ teaspoon garlic powder
       Parsley, chopped

Season squirrel with salt and pepper. Pour vegetable oil into a large skillet, and brown squirrel. Discard cooking oil. Mix remaining ingredients well, then pour over squirrel; cover and simmer for 40 to 50 minutes or until meat is tender. Garnish with parsley.

    Serve with baked beans or potato salad and coleslaw.

Squirrel in Orange Sauce

  2 pounds squirrel, cut up
    Salt and pepper
¼ cup butter or margarine
  2 tablespoons all-purpose flour
⅛ teaspoon ground cinnamon
    Dash of ground ginger
1½ cups fresh orange juice
½ cup blanched almonds, slivered
½ cup currants
  1 cup orange sections

Sprinkle pieces of squirrel with salt and pepper. Melt butter in a large, heavy skillet and brown squirrel. Remove squirrel from skillet and drain off all but 2 tablespoons of pan drippings. Blend flour, cinnamon, ginger, and ¼ teaspoon salt into drippings; cook over low heat, stirring constantly, until brown. Gradually add orange juice; cook until smooth and thickened, stirring constantly. Stir in slivered almonds and currants. Add squirrel to sauce; cover and cook over low heat for 30 minutes or until squirrel is tender. Add orange sections just before serving.

Serve with rice and hot bread.

Squirrel in Wine Sauce

2 squirrels, whole
Salt
Ground nutmeg
6 tablespoons butter or margarine, melted
2 tablespoons onion, minced
1 pound fresh mushrooms, quartered
⅔ cup dry white wine

½ cup cashew nuts
1 teaspoon cornstarch
2 tablespoons brandy
Carrot, shredded
Hot cooked rice

Sprinkle squirrels inside and out with salt and nutmeg. Pour melted butter into a large skillet and brown each side of squirrels. Add onion, mushrooms, wine, and cashews. Bring to a boil; reduce heat, cover, and simmer for 15 minutes. Remove squirrels to greased 2-quart casserole. Combine cornstarch and brandy; mix well and stir into skillet. Cook, stirring constantly, until thickened. Add mixture to squirrels. Bake at 350 degrees for 30 minutes or until meat is tender. Garnish with shredded carrot. Serve squirrels and sauce over rice.

Herb-Fried Squirrel

½ cup all-purpose flour
¾ teaspoon salt
¼ teaspoon paprika
¼ teaspoon ground thyme
¼ teaspoon ground marjoram
   Pinch freshly ground black pepper
2 squirrels, cut up
¼ cup buttermilk
   Vegetable oil

Combine dry ingredients; mix well. Dip pieces of squirrel in buttermilk; dredge in flour mixture, coating well. Pour oil 1 inch deep into skillet; add squirrel and cook over medium heat for 20 minutes or until golden brown, turning occasionally.
Serve with french fries, coleslaw, and hot biscuits.

Tasty Squirrel Casserole

1 10¾-ounce can condensed cream of chicken soup
⅔ cup milk
2 tablespoons onion, finely chopped
¼ teaspoon garlic powder
2 tablespoons Parmesan cheese, grated
⅛ teaspoon freshly ground white pepper
2 cups squirrel, cooked, deboned, and chopped
2 cups green tomato or zucchini, sliced
1 cup fresh mushrooms, sliced
⅔ cup buttered bread crumbs
¼ cup cashew nuts or almonds, chopped

Combine soup, milk, onion, garlic powder, cheese, and pepper in saucepan; mix well. Bring mixture to a boil over medium heat. Add squirrel, tomato or zucchini, and mushrooms and stir. Pour into an 11-by-7-inch baking dish. Sprinkle bread crumbs and nuts over top. Bake in preheated oven at 375 degrees for 25 minutes.

Squirrel Chowder

1 cup potatoes, peeled and cubed
½ cup onions, finely chopped
½ cup celery, chopped
3 cups milk
½ cup fresh mushrooms, chopped
1 cup cooked squirrel, chopped
1 teaspoon salt
⅛ teaspoon freshly ground white pepper
⅛ teaspoon ground nutmeg

Cook potatoes, onion, and celery in milk in a large saucepan for about 10 minutes or until tender; mash potatoes lightly. Add mushrooms, squirrel, and seasoning; stir well. Simmer, uncovered, for 5 minutes more.

Serve with freshly baked corn bread.

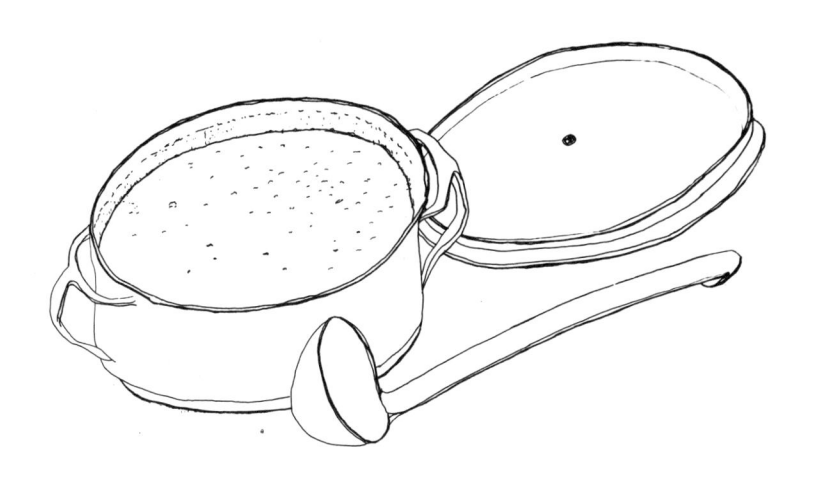

Groundhog

❧ Braised Groundhog and Bourbon Sauce

    1 cup all-purpose flour
    1 teaspoon thyme
    1 teaspoon paprika
    1 teaspoon freshly ground black pepper
    ¼ teaspoon cayenne
    1 teaspoon salt
    1 teaspoon garlic powder
2½ to 3 pounds groundhog, cut up
    1 cup milk
    ½ cup butter or margarine
    1 cup dry white wine
    1 teaspoon fresh lemon juice
    1 cup fresh mushrooms, sliced
    1 tablespoon parsley, finely chopped
    2 tablespoons Kentucky bourbon
    1 cup sour cream

Combine flour and other dry ingredients, except parsley, and mix well in a plastic bag. Dampen each piece of groundhog with ½ cup milk and drop into flour mixture one piece at a time, shaking the bag to thoroughly coat each piece. Melt butter in a large skillet over medium to high heat and brown each piece of groundhog thoroughly. Combine wine, lemon juice, and mushrooms and pour over pieces. Cover and simmer for 20 minutes. Remove groundhog from skillet; add parsley, bourbon, sour cream, and ½ cup milk to drippings; blend and heat to desired thickness. Pour part of sauce over groundhog and serve remainder in gravy boat.

Variations of Braised Groundhog

Mexicali Groundhog

Add the following ingredients to the flour mixture in the basic recipe.

2 teaspoons chili powder
1 teaspoon cumin
1 teaspoon oregano

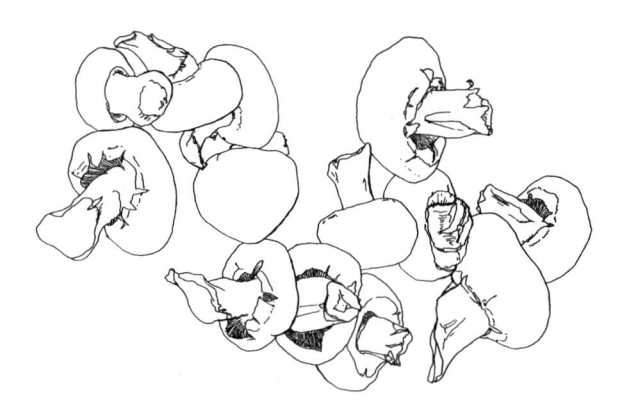

Turkey-Style Groundhog

Add the following ingredients to the flour mixture in the basic recipe.

½ teaspoon allspice
½ teaspoon sage
½ teaspoon coriander
½ teaspoon marjoram

ɤ Garlic-Flavored Fried Groundhog

¾ cup milk
3 eggs, beaten
4 cloves garlic, minced
5 to 6 pounds groundhog, cut up
1 cup all-purpose flour
2 cups fine bread crumbs
½ teaspoon garlic powder
½ teaspoon salt
¼ teaspoon freshly ground black pepper
Vegetable oil

Combine milk, eggs, garlic; set aside. Wash groundhog and pat dry; dredge in flour. Combine bread crumbs, garlic powder, salt, and pepper. Dip pieces of groundhog in egg mixture; then dredge in bread crumb mixture, coating well. Heat vegetable oil to 350 degrees in a large, heavy skillet. Cook groundhog in hot oil until golden brown. Drain groundhog on paper towels and place pieces on a rack in shallow baking pan. Bake at 350 degrees for 30 to 40 minutes or until done.

Serve with baked sweet potatoes and sourdough bread.

WILD GAME BIRDS

Wild Turkey

Roast Wild Turkey

1 12- to 14-pound wild turkey
Salt
Butter or margarine
Flour
Dressing (see following recipe)

Remove neck and giblets (gizzard, liver, and heart) from turkey and reserve for giblet gravy. Rinse bird thoroughly inside and out with cold water; pat dry. Sprinkle entire surface of bird lightly with salt, and rub breast, drumsticks, and wings with ½ cup butter until creamy and pat with ¼ cup flour.

Stuff neck cavity with small amount of dressing, fasten skin to back with skewer; lightly stuff large cavity. Tuck drumsticks under band of skin at tail and fold wing tips across back of bird.

Place bird on roasting rack in drip pan, breast side up. Insert meat thermometer in breast or thickest part of drumstick, making sure it does not touch the bone. Bake at 325 degrees for 1 hour or until bird begins to brown. Reduce heat to 300 degrees and bake for 20 minutes per pound (about 4 to 5 hours) or until thermometer reaches 185 degrees; bird will be very brown. Rotate pan one-half turn every 20 minutes and baste with drippings during entire baking time.

When bird is two-thirds done, open cavity and spread drumsticks; this will permit the inside of the thighs to be cooked sufficiently.

The bird is done when the thermometer reaches 185 degrees or when drumsticks can be moved up and down easily.

Remove bird from oven and let cool for 20 minutes before carving.

Serve with giblet gravy.

Wild Turkey Dressing

- ¾ cup shallots or onions, finely chopped
- 1½ cups celery, finely chopped
- ½ cup fresh coriander or parsley, finely chopped
- 1 cup butter or margarine, melted
- 12 cups soft bread crumbs
- 2 cups chestnuts or peanuts, boiled and hulled
- 1 tablespoon salt
- ½ teaspoon freshly ground black pepper
- ½ teaspoon marjoram
- 1 tablespoon rubbed sage
- ¼ teaspoon allspice
- 4½ cups water

Sauté shallots, celery, and coriander in butter in a large skillet until tender. Add remaining ingredients; mix well and spoon into the bird's cavities. Spoon remaining dressing into a greased baking dish and bake at 350 degrees for 45 minutes to 1 hour or until lightly browned.

This recipe may be cut in half for use with smaller birds.

Giblet Gravy

- 3 cups water
- 1 teaspoon salt

    Neck and giblets from 1 wild turkey
6 tablespoons all-purpose flour
    Water
    Salt
    Pepper

Combine water and salt in a medium saucepan; bring to a boil. Reduce heat, add neck and giblets, and simmer for 15 minutes. Remove liver and continue to simmer until remaining giblets are tender. Remove giblets from broth and discard neck; chop meat and return to broth.

Blend flour and small amounts of water into smooth paste; stir into broth. Cook, stirring constantly, until desired thickness is attained. Add salt and pepper to taste.

CURRANT-GLAZED WILD TURKEY

1 12- to 14-pound wild turkey
2 tablespoons salt
1 tablespoon fresh ginger root, grated
1 teaspoon cumin
½ teaspoon dried rosemary leaves
½ teaspoon dried tarragon leaves
½ teaspoon dried dill weed
½ teaspoon cayenne
1 bay leaf, crumbled
½ cup butter or margarine
1 tablespoon all-purpose flour
1 tablespoon honey
¼ cup port wine
   Currant Glaze

Remove neck and giblets (gizzard, liver, and heart) from turkey and reserve for giblet gravy. Rinse bird thoroughly inside and out with cold water; pat dry.

Make a mixture of salt, ginger root, and cumin. Rub cavity and skin with mixture. Place turkey in refrigerator and let stand overnight.

Remove bird from refrigerator and let stand at room temperature for 1 hour. Make mixture of remaining herbs. Rub skin and cavity with butter, then rub on herb mixture.

Tuck drumsticks under band of skin at tail. Fold wing tips across back of bird. Place bird on roasting rack, breast side up.

Combine flour and honey; stir well. Blend in port wine. Brush turkey with this mixture. Place bird on roasting rack in drip pan, breast side up. Insert meat thermometer in breast or thickest part of drumstick, making sure it does not touch the bone. Bake at 325 degrees for 1 hour or until bird begins to brown. Reduce heat to 300 degrees and bake for 20 minutes per pound (about 4 to 5 hours) or until thermometer reaches 185 degrees; turkey will be very brown. Rotate pan one-half turn every 20 minutes and baste with drippings during entire baking time.

When bird is two-thirds done, open cavity and spread drumsticks; this will permit the inside of the thighs to be cooked sufficiently.

The bird is done when the thermometer reaches 185 degrees or when drumsticks can be moved up and down easily.

Place bird on platter and brush with Currant Glaze.

Currant Glaze

    1 cup orange juice
    1½ tablespoons cornstarch
    1 cup currant jelly
    ½ cup sugar

Combine small amounts of orange juice with cornstarch in a small saucepan. Blend well; stir in jelly and sugar. Cook over low heat for 10 minutes or until thickened, stirring occasionally. Remove from heat and let cool before brushing on bird.

SIMPLE BROILED WILD TURKEY

    1 12- to 14-pound wild turkey, cut up
    2 sticks butter or margarine
    1 teaspoon salt
    ½ teaspoon freshly ground black pepper
    2 cups stock

Rub turkey with butter and sprinkle with salt and pepper; then place on a well-greased broiler, 2 inches from gas flame or 1 inch from electric coils. Broil for 20 minutes, turning occasionally, so all parts are evenly browned.

Place turkey in a baking pan and dot with butter, then add stock. Cover tightly and bake in preheated oven at 350 degrees for 30 minutes. Baste several times with liquids in the pan.

❦ SMOKED TURKEY AND RICE WITH PINEAPPLE SAUCE

½ cup green onions, tops included
½ teaspoon garlic, minced
6 tablespoons butter or margarine
4 small eggs, beaten
2 cups cooked white rice
2 cups cooked leftover turkey, chopped

Sauté onion and garlic in 2 tablespoons of butter in a skillet until the onion wilts. Remove from skillet and set aside in a bowl. Melt 2 tablespoons butter in the skillet and add eggs; fry over medium heat, stirring until they are solid and scrambled. Place eggs in bowl with onions and garlic.

Melt 2 tablespoons butter in skillet, add rice and turkey, then sauté for 3 minutes over medium heat, stirring occasionally. Stir in contents of bowl and fold in. When well heated, remove from burner, cover, and set aside.

Pineapple Sauce

1 cup cream
1 cup fresh mushrooms, thinly sliced
1 teaspoon curry powder
½ cup pineapple juice
¼ teaspoon ground ginger
1 cup pineapple chunks

Combine all ingredients in a saucepan; bring to a boil, reduce heat, and simmer for 10 minutes.

Serve sauce ladled over smoked turkey and rice.

Wild Duck

Wild ducks should never be stuffed, but usually a slice of orange, a slice of onion, or ribs of celery, or a combination of all three, is placed in the cavity to add to the flavor.

Wild ducks are normally roasted at low temperatures for 2 to 3 hours or at a high temperature for a short period and served rare. The latter method produces a juicier, more tender, and more flavorful bird.

Rare duck is sometimes referred to as "bloody" duck; the recipe for Bloody Wild Duck with Orange Sauce has been included for those who like their duck prepared this way.

Wine and Bourbon Duck

4 small wild ducks, 1½ pounds each, halved
8 bacon strips
Olive oil
Flour
2 medium onions, thinly sliced
2 cloves garlic, minced
½ teaspoon thyme
2 tablespoons fresh parsley, finely minced
2 bay leaves, crumbled
1 cup sweet bell pepper, ½-inch cubes
½ teaspoon freshly ground black pepper
1 cup dry red wine
3 tablespoons Kentucky bourbon
1 teaspoon salt
6 carrots, cut into 2-inch sections

Place duck halves skin side up in a large, deep roasting pan. Fasten one bacon strip on each duck half with toothpicks. Sprinkle ducks lightly with olive oil and then flour. Add onion, garlic, thyme, parsley, and bay leaves. Bake in preheated oven at 350 degrees for 1½ hours.

Remove duck from roasting pan and place carefully in large, deep pot. Add remaining ingredients. Place the pot on high heat and bring to a simmer, then reduce heat to low and simmer for ½ to 1 hour. Duck should be tender. Serve duck with sauce ladled over each portion.

Serve with candied sweet potatoes, steamed cauliflower, and hot rolls.

Roast Wild Duck with Herbs

8 small wild ducks, about 1½ pounds each
Salt
2 large onions, quartered
8 bay leaves, whole
1 quart dry red wine
½ cup vegetable oil
2 cups water
1 teaspoon freshly ground black pepper
½ teaspoon cayenne
½ teaspoon dried thyme
1 teaspoon garlic, minced
¼ cup butter or margarine
1 teaspoon ground coriander
½ cup onion, finely chopped
2 tablespoons parsley, minced

Sprinkle ducks with salt. Place 1 onion quarter and one bay leaf in the cavity of each duck; then place ducks breast side down in a large roaster.

Combine remaining ingredients in a saucepan and bring mixture to a boil; remove from heat and pour over ducks. Cover and bake at 350 degrees for 3 hours or until ducks feel tender when pierced with a two-tined fork. Baste occasionally with pan drippings.

Lemon-Roast Wild Duck

   2 large wild ducks, whole
  ½ stick butter or margarine, softened
    Salt and pepper
   1 medium onion, halved
   4 bacon strips, cut into halves
  ¼ cup olive oil
   1 cup dry white wine
    Juice of 1 lemon
   1 cup water; more if necessary
   1 cup chicken stock
   1 teaspoon dried thyme

Rub ducks with butter; salt and pepper inside and out. Place onion half inside cavities. Lay bacon strips across ducks and place in roasting pan.

Combine olive oil, wine, lemon juice, water, stock, and thyme. Baste ducks with mixture before and several times during baking.

Place ducks breast side down. Bake in preheated oven at 325 degrees for about 3 to 4 hours. Turn breast side up and continue roasting for 30 minutes or until browned.

❦ Bloody Wild Duck with Orange Sauce

    2 small ducks, about 1½ to 2 pounds each
    ½ stick butter
       Salt and pepper
    ¼ cup vegetable oil
    ¼ cup dry white wine
       Juice of 1 lemon
    ½ cup chicken stock

Rub ducks with butter inside and out and sprinkle with salt and pepper. Place ducks in a roasting pan. Bake in preheated oven at 425 degrees for 30 minutes. Baste several times while baking with a mixture of vegetable oil, wine, lemon juice, and stock.
    Serve with Orange Sauce.

Orange Sauce

    ⅔ cup sugar
    2 teaspoons cornstarch
    ¼ teaspoon salt
    1 cup boiling water
    ½ cup dry white wine
    1 teaspoon olive oil
    1 teaspoon lemon juice
    ½ cup orange rind, grated
    1 cup orange juice

Mix sugar, cornstarch, and salt in a saucepan. Pour boiling water over mixture, stirring constantly. Simmer over medium heat until thick and clear. Add rest of ingredients, mix well, and remove from heat.
    Serve ladled over duck.

Orange-Glazed Wild Duck

    3 small wild ducks, 1½ to 2 pounds, halved
    Salt and pepper
    Peel of 1 orange
    ½ cup currant jelly
    ¼ cup white wine
    ¼ cup orange juice
    2 tablespoons fresh lemon juice
    2 teaspoons dry mustard
    1 teaspoon paprika
    ½ teaspoon ground ginger
    1 teaspoon cornstarch

Sprinkle duck halves with salt and pepper.

Chop remaining ingredients in a blender or a food processor until orange rind is finely cut up; pour into a saucepan and simmer, stirring constantly for five minutes.

Coat duck halves thoroughly with orange glaze. Arrange duck halves, skin side up, on a lightly greased grill, about 4 inches from hot coals. Cook for 45 to 55 minutes or until meat is no longer pink near bone; turn and baste frequently with orange glaze.

Duck Breast in Wine Sauce

    3 large whole duck breasts, halved, boned, and skinned
    Salt and pepper
    Ground nutmeg
    6 tablespoons butter or margarine
    ½ cup onion, minced

1 pound fresh mushroom caps
2½ cups dry white wine
  1 cup cashew nuts, whole
  1 tablespoon cornstarch
    Hot cooked rice

Sprinkle duck breasts with salt, pepper, and nutmeg. Melt butter in a heavy skillet, add duck, and brown each side. Add onion, mushrooms, 2 cups wine, and cashews. Bring to a boil. Reduce heat, cover, and simmer for 15 minutes. Remove duck pieces.

Combine cornstarch and remaining wine; mix well and stir into skillet. Cook over low heat until thickened, stirring constantly.

Serve duck and sauce over rice.

Herb-Fried Wild Duck

1½ cups all-purpose flour
2¼ teaspoons salt
  1 teaspoon paprika
  1 teaspoon ground thyme
  1 teaspoon ground marjoram
  ½ teaspoon freshly ground black pepper
  1 cup buttermilk
    Vegetable oil
  3 large duck breasts, halved, boned, and skinned

Combine first 6 ingredients and mix well. Dip each piece of duck in buttermilk; then dredge in flour mixture, coating well. Heat 1-inch-deep oil in a skillet; add duck pieces and cook over medium heat for 20 minutes or until golden brown, turning occasionally. Drain pieces on paper towel.

Serve with fresh lima beans, field peas, pickled beets, and corn bread sticks.

Barbecued Wild Duck Breast

8 wild duck breasts, split, boned, and skinned

Barbecue Sauce

    1 large onion, sliced
    Vegetable oil, for sautéing
    ½ cup tomato sauce
    ¼ cup brown sugar
    ¼ cup dry red wine
    1 tablespoon prepared mustard
    ⅛ teaspoon freshly ground black pepper
    ⅛ teaspoon cayenne
    ½ teaspoon salt
    ¼ cup vegetable oil

Soak duck breasts in saltwater for 3 to 4 hours. Remove and dry with paper towels.

To make barbecue sauce, sauté onions in oil. Place onions and remaining ingredients in a blender or food processor and blend.

Place duck breasts in a stainless-steel or porcelain bowl and brush on sauce. Let stand in refrigerator overnight.

Remove duck breasts from refrigerator and grill over slow-burning coals for 5 to 8 minutes on each side. Brush on additional sauce several times while cooking.

Kentucky-Style Wild Duck

    ½ cup vegetable oil
    1 large duck, 3 to 4 pounds, cut up
    1 cup chicken broth
    1 teaspoon paprika
    1 cup water
    1 teaspoon fresh lemon juice

1 medium onion, finely chopped
1 tablespoon sugar
2 tablespoons Kentucky bourbon
¼ teaspoon cayenne
¼ teaspoon freshly ground black pepper
1 clove garlic, minced
½ pound mushrooms, thinly sliced
½ cup dry white wine
3 cups hot cooked rice

Heat vegetable oil in a large skillet and brown duck on all sides; pour off drippings. Add remaining ingredients, except mushrooms and wine. Simmer covered for 90 minutes or until tender. Add extra water if needed. Remove duck to hot platter.
Add mushrooms and wine to the skillet and heat, stirring constantly. Place duck and sauce over rice.
Serve with hominy, green salad, and hot rolls.

WILD DUCK PÂTÉ

4 cups cooked leftover duck meat
½ cup celery, cut up
½ cup green onions, cut up
¼ cup sweet green peppers
2 tablespoons fresh lemon juice
1 teaspoon salt
½ teaspoon Tabasco sauce
½ cup mayonnaise
1 tablespoon Worcestershire sauce
¼ teaspoon freshly ground black pepper

Combine all ingredients in a blender or food processor and blend for 1 minute or until smooth. Spoon into a 1-quart mold; chill for 4 hours or overnight.
Serve with your favorite cracker.

Wild Duck Tidbits and Rice with Sauce

- 8 wild duck breasts, boned, skinned, and cut into 1-inch cubes
- Vegetable oil
- 3 tablespoons butter or margarine
- ½ cup onion, chopped
- 2 cups white rice, cooked
- 1 teaspoon salt
- ¼ teaspoon freshly ground black pepper
- 2 tablespoons sweet green peas

Sauté duck cubes in vegetable oil over medium heat for 7 minutes on each side. Remove duck from skillet and drain on paper towels. Drain oil from skillet, then add butter. Sauté onions over medium heat until tender. Add rice, salt, pepper, and duck cubes. Stir over medium heat for 3 minutes. Add peas and stir lightly for 2 minutes. Serve with sauce ladled over top.

Sauce

- 2 tablespoons butter or margarine
- ¼ cup onion, finely chopped
- 2 tablespoons all-purpose flour
- 1 cup wild duck or chicken stock
- ½ teaspoon dried marjoram
- ½ teaspoon salt
- ¼ teaspoon freshly ground black pepper
- ¼ cup brandy
- ½ cup heavy cream

Melt butter in a saucepan over medium heat; add onion and sauté until golden brown. Gradually stir in flour, keeping the mixture smooth. Then add stock slowly and cook over low heat until sauce thickens. Add remaining ingredients and simmer for 5 minutes.

Wild Goose

Goose with Fruit Stuffing

- 2 cups prunes, pitted
- 2 cups currants
- 2 cups fresh peaches, diced
- 2 cups dried apricots
- 2 cups dried apples
- Sherry
- 1 10-pound goose
- Salt and pepper to taste
- 2 fresh pears
- 1 cup dry or toasted bread crumbs
- 8 whole cloves
- ¼ teaspoon nutmeg
- ½ teaspoon cinnamon
- ½ teaspoon ginger
- ¾ cup brandy

Place prunes, currants, peaches, apricots, and apples in a stainless-steel or porcelain bowl; add enough sherry to cover. Let stand overnight in refrigerator. Sprinkle goose inside and out with salt and pepper. Peel, core, and dice pears; add to rest of fruit. Mix fruit, bread crumbs, and spices; stuff into cavity of goose; truss. Place goose, breast side up, in roasting pan. Bake, covered, in preheated oven at 350 degrees for about 30 minutes per pound (15 minutes per pound if goose has been parboiled), draining off fat occasionally and basting frequently with brandy. Remove cover for the last 30 minutes of baking.

Roast Goose

    1 goose, about 8 pounds
    Salt and pepper
    1 bay leaf
    2 orange slices
    ½ teaspoon garlic, minced
    4 bacon slices
    1 cup chicken broth
    ½ cup onion, finely chopped
    ½ cup fresh parsley, finely chopped
    1 teaspoon thyme
    1½ cups water (more if necessary)

Parboil goose until tender.

Sprinkle goose inside and out with salt and pepper. Place bay leaf, orange slices, and garlic in cavity. Tie legs together with heavy string. Turn wings under. Cover breast with bacon slices and fasten to bird with toothpicks. Place goose breast side up in baking pan and add remaining ingredients. Bake at 350 degrees, allowing 15 minutes per pound. It takes about 2 hours to bake an 8-pound goose. Baste frequently with liquids in pan.

Red cabbage is an excellent side dish, as is white rice.

Fricasseed Goose

Goose (about 6 pounds), cut into serving-sized pieces
1 teaspoon garlic powder
2 teaspoons salt
¼ teaspoon freshly ground black pepper
2 teaspoons ground ginger
6 cups boiling water
1 large onion, sliced
2 stalks celery, sliced into 2-inch sections
4 tablespoons all-purpose flour
2 cups strained goose broth
1 tablespoon parsley, chopped

Sprinkle goose pieces with a mixture of garlic powder, salt, pepper, and ginger. Place in stainless-steel or porcelain dish; cover and let stand 12 hours or overnight in refrigerator.

Remove goose pieces from refrigerator and place in a heavy saucepan or kettle; cover with boiling water. Add onion and celery, cover, and simmer gently for 2½ to 3½ hours, or until goose is tender, adding more water if necessary.

Stir flour into ½-cup cooled broth, then generally add 1½ cups broth and mix thoroughly. Bring to a boil; cook until thickened and smooth, stirring constantly for about 2 minutes; continue cooking for 4 or 5 minutes; add parsley.

Arrange goose on platter and pour sauce over pieces. Garnish with sprigs of parsley and orange slices.

✣ Goose Cracklings

Skin of 1 goose
Salt
1 cup cold water

Remove the skin from a goose and cut it into 1-by-1½-inch squares; sprinkle with salt and let stand in cool place or refrigerator for 12 hours. Wash well and dry with paper towels.

Place skin and water to cover in a quart saucepan and simmer for 1 hour. Drain and sauté slowly to prevent scorching. For chewy cracklings, remove them as soon as fat is clear; for crisp cracklings, leave them in hot fat until well browned and then place in a 400-degree oven for a few minutes. Drain well on paper towels. Pour goose fat into jars and cover; when cool, refrigerate for later use.

Serve goose cracklings with your favorite dip, cheese spread, or pâté. They're great at parties.

Pheasant

❧ Barbecued Marinated Pheasant

½ teaspoon dried basil
½ teaspoon oregano
2 tablespoons brown sugar
¾ cup catsup
¼ cup soy sauce
½ teaspoon garlic, minced
  Juice of 1 small lemon
½ teaspoon salt
¼ teaspoon freshly ground black pepper
½ teaspoon cayenne
1 pheasant, 2½ to 3 pounds, cut into serving-sized pieces

Combine first 10 ingredients in a stainless-steel or porcelain bowl and mix well. Add pheasant pieces, cover, and marinate overnight in the refrigerator, turning once or twice.
  Preheat oven to 300 degrees.
  Place pheasant and marinade in baking dish or casserole. Cover and bake for 1 hour.
  Serve pheasant, bathed in cooking juices, on a heated platter.

❧ Raisin-and-Pecan-Stuffed Pheasant

- ½ cup butter or margarine, melted
- 1 cup bread crumbs
- ½ cup pecans, coarsely chopped
- ½ cup raisins
- 2 pheasants, 2½ to 3 pounds each
- Salt and pepper
- Butter
- 3 tablespoons flour
- 1½ cups water
- ½ cup sherry
- 1 teaspoon thyme
- ½ cup parsley, finely chopped
- ½ cup onion, finely chopped
- 1 teaspoon garlic, minced

Pour melted butter over bread crumbs; add pecans and raisins and toss lightly. Stuff pheasants' cavities with pecan and raisin mixture and truss.

Sprinkle birds with salt and pepper; rub with butter, then sprinkle with flour. Place birds in roasting pan and bake, uncovered, at 400 degrees until browned. Reduce heat to 350 degrees. Add hot water, sherry, thyme, parsley, onion, and garlic to roasting pan. Bake, covered, for 1 hour or until juices run clear from thigh when birds are pierced with a two-tined fork.

Serve with baked candied yams.

Roast Pheasant with Vegetables

Salt and pepper
2 pheasants, 2 to 2½ pounds each
½ stick butter or margarine
1 cup chicken stock
½ teaspoon thyme
2 smoked bacon strips
3 carrots, cut into 2-inch sections
1 large onion, sliced
2 stalks celery, cut into 1-inch sections
2 small zucchini, halved lengthwise
2 large potatoes, peeled, pared, and cut into 1½-inch cubes
¼ cup olive oil
Juice of 1 lemon
½ cup dry white wine
1 pound fresh mushrooms
½ cup parsley, finely chopped
½ teaspoon garlic, minced

Salt and pepper pheasants inside and out and rub with butter. Place birds in roasting pan; bake in preheated oven at 400 degrees, uncovered, until skin is brown.

Remove roasting pan from oven and add stock and thyme. Fasten bacon strips across each bird's breast with toothpicks. Place carrots, onion, celery, zucchini, and potatoes around pheasants. Mix olive oil, lemon juice, and wine in small dish for basting. Baste before returning to oven and several times during baking. Cover and bake for 1 hour at 350 degrees. Remove from oven, add remaining ingredients, and bake, covered, for 30 minutes longer.

Pheasant Breast with Mushroom Sauce

Vegetable oil
8 pheasant breasts, split, boned, and skinned

Mushroom Sauce

    2 tablespoons butter
    1½ pounds fresh mushrooms, thinly sliced
    2 tablespoons all-purpose flour
    1 cup milk
    1 cup heavy cream
    2 tablespoons dry red wine
    ½ teaspoon salt
    ¼ teaspoon freshly ground black pepper
    Hot cooked rice

Put oil in a large skillet and brown pheasant breasts on all sides over medium heat. Drain off oil and set aside.

Melt butter and sauté mushrooms in a saucepan for about 10 minutes. Add flour and blend well; gradually pour in milk and cream. Cook over low heat until mixture is thickened. Stir in wine and seasonings.

Pour saucepan mixture into skillet over the breasts. Simmer covered for 30 minutes.

Serve breasts on rice with mushroom sauce ladled over top.

Quail and Other Small Game Birds

All small birds may be substituted for one another in the following recipes; however, the smaller the bird, the shorter the cooking time.

Roast Quail

   8 quail
      Salt
      Freshly ground black pepper
      Butter or margarine
      All-purpose flour
½ cup dry sherry
¼ cup butter or margarine, melted
1 tablespoon fresh lemon juice
¼ teaspoon paprika
¼ cup water
2 tablespoons Worcestershire sauce

Sprinkle quail with salt and pepper inside and out. Place 2 tablespoons butter inside cavity of each bird. Rub birds with a mixture of equal amounts of butter and flour.

Combine sherry, melted butter, lemon juice, paprika, water, and Worcestershire sauce and mix well. Use mixture for basting birds.

Bake birds at 275 degrees for 1 hour, basting frequently.

Serve with fried green tomatoes topped with cheese sauce, parsleyed turnips, and baby carrots.

Kentucky Stuffed Quail with Cream Sauce

8 to 10 quail, whole
Salt and pepper
Butter or margarine, melted

Dressing

½ cup onion, finely chopped
½ cup fresh coriander, finely chopped
½ pound chicken livers
⅓ cup butter or margarine
½ teaspoon salt
¼ teaspoon black pepper, freshly ground
¼ cup fresh parsley, finely minced
3 cups corn bread stuffing
⅓ cup water
1 large egg, lightly beaten
½ teaspoon ground sage
¼ teaspoon thyme
½ teaspoon dried marjoram

Sauce

2 tablespoons butter or margarine
2 tablespoons all-purpose flour
1 cup chicken stock
½ cup heavy cream
¼ teaspoon freshly ground white pepper
½ teaspoon salt

Rinse quail and dry thoroughly. Sprinkle birds lightly with salt and pepper, then place them in a baking dish and bake in preheated oven at 450 degrees for 20 minutes. Remove quail from oven and let cool.

Sauté onion, coriander, and chicken livers in butter for 15 minutes. Add remaining ingredients and mix well. Cook for 10 minutes longer over very low heat.

Lightly stuff quail cavities with small amounts of dressing. Close cavity openings with skewers or sew with strong white thread.

Brush quail with melted butter, return to the oven, and bake at 450 degrees for 30 minutes longer.

Prepare the sauce while quail are baking. Melt butter in a saucepan over medium heat. Gradually stir in flour until mixture is smooth. Add stock and cook over low heat until thickened. Add remaining ingredients and mix well, then cook for 10 minutes longer. Serve quail with sauce spooned over top.

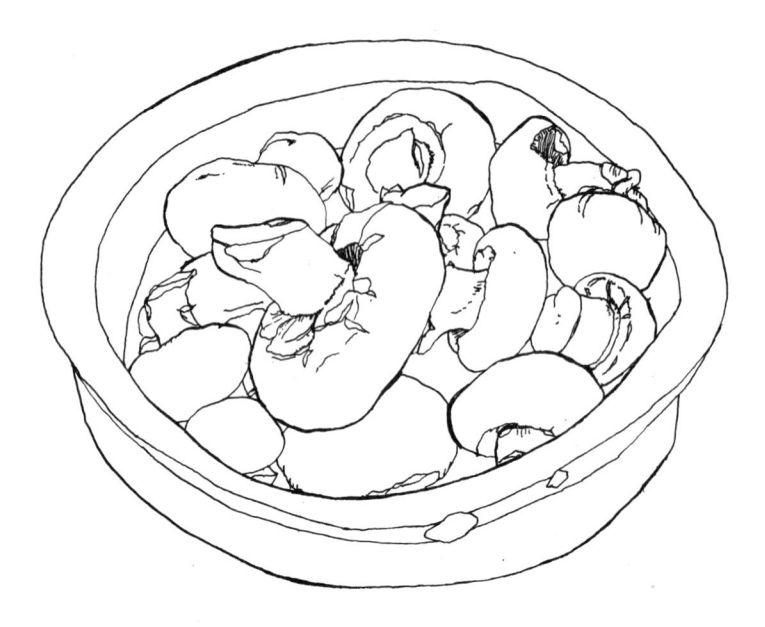

Quail Supreme

- 1 cup all-purpose flour
- ½ teaspoon garlic salt
- 1 teaspoon paprika
- ¼ teaspoon freshly ground black pepper
- ½ cup butter or margarine
- 8 quail
- ½ cup dry white wine
- ½ cup water
- 1 teaspoon fresh lemon juice
- 1 tablespoon parsley, finely chopped
- 2 tablespoons brandy
- 1 cup fresh mushrooms, sliced
- ½ cup milk
- 1 cup sour cream
- Cashew nuts (optional)

Combine flour, garlic salt, paprika, and pepper; coat quail with mixture. Melt butter in skillet and brown birds on all sides. Combine wine, water, lemon juice, and parsley and pour over quail. Cover and simmer for 20 minutes. Remove quail from skillet. Add brandy, mushrooms, milk, and sour cream to skillet and blend with pan drippings; heat to desired thickness. Pour part of sauce over quail and serve remainder in gravy boat. Garnish with cashew nuts, if desired.

Quail Sauterne

- 1 tablespoon all-purpose flour
- 6 quail, whole, about 3 to 4 pounds
- Salt
- Red pepper
- 1 cup onion, finely chopped
- ½ cup sweet bell pepper, cut into 1-inch cubes
- 1 cup parsley, finely chopped
- 1 clove garlic, minced
- 1 lemon, peeled and cut into ¼-inch chunks
- 4 pounds fresh small mushroom caps
- 1 cup water
- 1 cup sauterne wine

Place 1 tablespoon flour in a 14-by-20-inch oven cooking bag; shake to coat well. Place bag in a 14-by-20-by-2-inch baking dish.

Sprinkle quail with salt and pepper. Place quail in bag. Add remaining ingredients on top of quail. Close bag with nylon tie. Punch 8 holes in top of bag with a two-tined fork. Bake in preheated oven at 350 degrees for 1 hour.

Grandma Rosa's Stuffed Quail with Tomato Sauce

    8 quail
       Salt and pepper
       Dressing (see following recipe)
       Vegetable oil
  ¼ cup onion, finely chopped
  ¼ cup sweet bell pepper, finely chopped
  1 clove garlic, minced
  1 teaspoon salt
  ½ teaspoon brown sugar
  2 cups stewed tomatoes, chopped
  ¾ teaspoon dried thyme leaves
  3 tablespoons vegetable oil
  ¼ teaspoon red pepper
      Parmesan cheese (optional)

Sprinkle entire surface of birds lightly with salt and pepper. Lightly stuff cavity with small amounts of dressing; close cavity openings with skewers.

    Heat ½-inch-deep vegetable oil in large skillet. Brown quail on all sides. Drain oil from skillet. Add remaining ingredients to birds. Add water to fill skillet two-thirds full. Cover and simmer for 2½ hours.

    Serve with tomato sauce in separate dish or over birds. Sprinkle with grated Parmesan cheese, if desired.

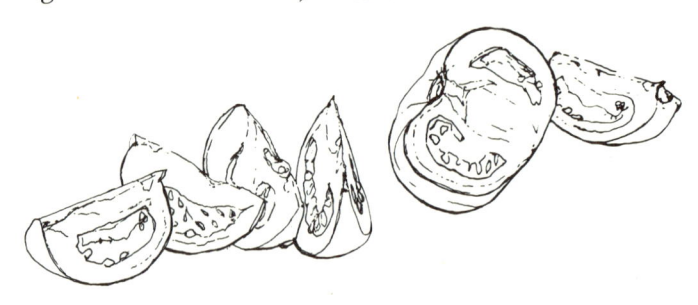

Dressing

- 4 cups bread crumbs
- ¼ cup onion, finely chopped
- ¼ cup raisins
- ½ cup blanched almonds, whole
- 1 cup mozzarella cheese, shredded
- ¼ teaspoon marjoram
- ¼ teaspoon thyme
- ½ cup butter or margarine, melted
- ½ teaspoon salt
- ⅛ teaspoon basil
- ⅛ teaspoon oregano
- ⅛ teaspoon sage
- ⅛ teaspoon savory
- ⅛ teaspoon rosemary

Combine all ingredients and mix well.

Tomato Sauce

- 1 cup tomatoes
- ¼ cup onion, finely chopped
- 1 tablespoon parsley, finely chopped
- 1 bay leaf, crumbled
- 2 tablespoons butter or margarine
- 2 tablespoons all-purpose flour
- ½ teaspoon salt
- ¼ teaspoon pepper

Put tomatoes, onion, parsley, and bay leaf in a saucepan; cook gently for 20 minutes, then rub through a sieve. Press all the pulp possible through the sieve and scrape off all that clings to the underside. Melt butter in another pan, add flour, and stir until smooth; stir in strained tomato slowly, to prevent the sauce from becoming lumpy. Bring to a boil and cook for 5 minutes; add salt and pepper and serve.

Famous Old-Style Quail

2 eggs
½ cup milk
¼ teaspoon turmeric
1 teaspoon salt
½ teaspoon freshly ground black pepper
Pinch cayenne
6 to 8 quail, halved
¼ cup vegetable oil
¼ cup onion, finely chopped
1 clove garlic, minced
¼ cup fresh coriander or parsley, chopped
½ cup white wine
¼ teaspoon cinnamon
¼ teaspoon paprika
1 cup sour cream
¼ cup cashew nuts, chopped
¼ cup almonds, chopped

Blend together eggs, milk, turmeric, salt, pepper, and cayenne in a shallow dish. Dip quail halves in mixture. Heat oil in large skillet. Brown birds on both sides. Remove quail from skillet and drain oil, leaving 2 tablespoons. Sauté onion, garlic, and coriander until tender.

Add wine, cinnamon, paprika, and sour cream, stirring constantly. Add quail, cover, and simmer for 5 minutes.

Remove quail to serving dish and garnish with cashews and almonds. Serve excess gravy in gravy boat.

Little Deviled Birds

6 quail, whole, about 3 to 4 pounds
1 cup butter or margarine
6 teaspoons prepared mustard
3 teaspoons salt
4 teaspoons vinegar
1 teaspoon paprika
   Buttered bread crumbs

Place quail in well-greased baking pan and broil for 8 minutes, then remove from the broiler.

Mix butter, mustard, salt, vinegar, and paprika in a bowl. Spread mustard mixture over birds, then sprinkle quail with buttered bread crumbs.

Bake quail in preheated oven at 350 degrees for 1 hour or until birds are tender and bread crumbs are browned.

Quail Potpie

    6 quail
    Salt and pepper
    Flour for dredging
    2 tablespoons butter or margarine
    1 stalk celery, cut into ½-inch sections
    3 carrots, cut into ½-inch sections
    1 tablespoon all-purpose flour
    Water
    ½ cup sweet peas
    1 teaspoon salt
    ¼ teaspoon freshly ground black pepper
    ½ cup dry white wine
    Pie dough for six pies

Remove breasts and legs from birds, sprinkle with salt and pepper, dredge with flour, and sauté in butter for 3 minutes on one side; turn and sauté for 4 minutes on the other side. Remove breasts and legs from skillet and set aside.

Cut backs of birds into pieces and place in saucepan; add celery, carrots, and enough water to cover. Cook over medium-low heat for 1 hour. Drain stock from saucepan into a mixing bowl and thicken with flour diluted with enough cold water to pour easily. Add peas, salt, pepper, and wine to sauce.

Use 1 9-inch pie plate for each bird. Line each plate with dough and brown in oven. Place 1 breast in each pie, add enough sauce for moisture, and cover with pie crust, making 2 incisions for 2 legs to extend through (resembling a whole bird inside the pie). Bake in preheated oven at 350 degrees until pie crust is browned and birds are heated through.

❧ Bluegrass Quail with Wine Sauce

- 10 quail, cut up, about 5 pounds
- ¼ cup cognac
- ⅓ cup all-purpose flour
- 1 teaspoon salt
- ¼ teaspoon freshly ground black pepper
- ½ teaspoon turmeric
- ¼ teaspoon coriander seed
- ¼ cup vegetable oil
- 1½ cups water
- 2½ cups dry white wine
- 1 clove garlic, crushed
- Sprig parsley
- ½ teaspoon peppercorns
- Sprig thyme
- 1 bay leaf
- ½ cup onion, finely chopped
- 1 pound fresh mushroom caps, whole

Place quail pieces in large skillet. Pour cognac over quail; ignite, then cover with a lid to extinguish flame. Mix flour, salt, pepper, turmeric, and coriander seed. Remove quail from skillet and dredge in flour mixture. Heat oil in skillet and lightly brown quail. Remove quail to baking dish.

Add water to 2 tablespoons drippings in skillet; heat, stirring until browned particles are loosened. Mix in wine and garlic, then pour over quail in baking dish. Tie parsley, peppercorns, thyme, and bay leaf in cheesecloth and add to quail. Cover and bake in preheated oven at 275 degrees for 1 hour. Remove cheesecloth from baking dish.

Sauté onions and mushrooms and add to quail. Cover and bake for 20 to 30 minutes longer or until quail are tender. Serve on hot platter with wine sauce.

Quail with Yellow Rice

   5 quail, halved, about 2½ pounds
   ½ cup butter or margarine
   1 cup yellow rice, uncooked
   1 pound fresh mushroom caps, whole
   ½ cup dry sherry
   1 teaspoon turmeric
   1 clove garlic, minced
     Dash freshly ground black pepper
     Dash cayenne
     Pinch rosemary
2½ cups boiling water
1½ teaspoons salt

Brown quail halves on both sides in hot butter; then put them in a 2-quart casserole. Sprinkle rice over and around quail; add mushrooms. Mix remaining ingredients and pour over quail. Cover and bake in a moderate oven (275 degrees) for about 1 hour.

Bryant County Quail

  10 quail, halved
   ¼ cup vegetable oil
  3½ cups sliced pineapple, canned, reserve liquid
   1 teaspoon garlic, minced
   1 teaspoon salt
   1 teaspoon ginger
   ½ cup sugar
   2 tablespoons cornstarch
   1 cup white wine
   ½ cup cashew nuts, coarsely chopped
   ½ cup green onion tops, chopped
     Hot cooked rice

Brown quail halves in oil on both sides. Drain oil from skillet and add pineapple cut into quarters, half the pineapple syrup from the can, garlic, salt, and ginger. Cover and cook over low heat for 1 hour. Remove quail from skillet and set aside.

Combine sugar, cornstarch, remaining pineapple syrup, and wine in skillet; cook over medium heat until thickened. Stir in cashews and onion tops.

Place quail on rice in serving dish; top with sauce and serve.

Quail Pâté

6 to 7 pounds quail, halved or cut up
1 tablespoon dried parsley
1 teaspoon thyme
1 teaspoon garlic, minced
2 stalks celery, cut into 1-inch pieces
½ cup onion, coarsely chopped
1½ teaspoons salt
¼ teaspoon pepper
1 sweet green bell pepper, coarsely chopped
4 scallions, cut up
4 stalks celery, cut up
Juice of 1 lemon
1 teaspoon salt
½ teaspoon Tabasco sauce
1 tablespoon soy sauce
½ cup mayonnaise

Combine first 8 ingredients in a large pot, cover with water, and bring to a boil; reduce heat, cover, and simmer for 1 hour or until meat is tender. Remove quail, cool, and debone.

Place quail meat and remaining ingredients in a blender or food processor and blend for 1 minute or until smooth.

Put meat in a 1-quart mold and chill for at least 2 hours, but preferably overnight. Yields about 4 cups.

Serve with your favorite cracker.

Quail Liver Pâté

    2 tablespoons butter or margarine
    2 tablespoons onion, finely minced
    2 cups quail or other game bird livers
    4 tablespoons dry red wine
    ¼ cup whipping cream
    ¼ teaspoon pepper
    ¼ teaspoon ground thyme
    ½ cup butter, melted
    ½ teaspoon salt
    ⅛ teaspoon paprika
    ⅛ teaspoon ground allspice

Melt butter in a skillet and sauté onions and livers until both are tender. Place cooked onions, livers, and remaining ingredients in a blender or food processor, and blend for 1 minute or until smooth. Put pâté into molds and chill in refrigerator for at least 2 hours, but preferably overnight. Yields 2½ cups.

Serve with your favorite cracker.

Hearty Quail Stew

    1 cup potatoes, diced
    2 cups cooked leftover quail meat, diced
    1 cup frozen lima beans
    1 cup whole-kernel corn
    ½ cup onion, chopped
    2 cups quail stock
    1 cup stewed tomatoes

1 teaspoon salt
¼ teaspoon ginger
¼ teaspoon freshly ground black pepper
½ cup celery, cut into ½-inch sections
1 cup carrots, cut into ½-inch sections

Combine all ingredients in a 3-quart pot; bring to a boil. Reduce heat and simmer for 1 hour or until thickened to desired consistency.

Smoked Quail Salad

2 smoked quail
1 cup celery, diced
 Salt and pepper to taste
4 tablespoons vegetable oil
2 tablespoons vinegar
 Mayonnaise dressing
 Lettuce
1 cucumber, sliced
1 large tomato, cut into wedges
½ cup mild cheddar cheese, grated
½ cup ripe pitted olives
2 hard-boiled eggs, sliced

After removing all skin and gristle, cut quail into julienne strips and toss with remaining ingredients, except eggs, for a chef's salad. Garnish with eggs.

Open-Faced Quail Sandwich

　1　10½-ounce can condensed cream of chicken soup
　1　pound smoked quail, sliced
　8　slices toasted white bread
　1　cup cashew nuts
　　　Salt and pepper to taste

Place soup in a skillet and thin down with milk or water to the consistency of thick gravy. Cook over medium heat until bubbly, then add quail, reduce heat, and simmer for 5 minutes. Place 2 slices of toast on 4 plates and spoon gravy and quail on top; sprinkle cashews over top. Salt and pepper to taste.

Baked Dove and Cashew Gravy

　8　doves, whole
　　　Salt
　　　Red pepper
　1　stick butter or margarine
　½　cup onion, finely chopped
　1　cup chicken stock
　½　cup dry white wine
　1　teaspoon dried thyme
　¼　cup fresh parsley, finely chopped
　¼　cup pan drippings
　⅓　cup all-purpose flour
　¾　cup milk
　¾　cup water
　　　Salt and pepper
　1　cup cashew nuts, halved

Sprinkle doves with salt and pepper. Rub birds with butter. Place birds in heavy roaster, bake, uncovered, in preheated oven at 400 degrees until browned. Remove pan from oven. Add onion, stock, wine, thyme, and parsley to roaster. Cover, return to oven, and bake at 300 degrees for 1½ hours, or until tender, basting every 15 minutes with pan juices.

Remove birds from pan; place on warm platter. Place ¼ cup drippings from roaster in a skillet; cook over medium heat and stir in flour until it turns a rich dark brown. Combine milk and water and pour into skillet; stir quickly until it thickens and bubbles. Season with salt and pepper to taste and stir in cashews.

Serve with freshly baked biscuits.

❧ Dove and Gravy

    12 doves, about 3 pounds
    Salt and pepper
    ½ cup butter or margarine
    2 tablespoons Worcestershire sauce
    ½ cup dry white wine
    1 teaspoon dried thyme
    ½ cup fresh parsley, finely minced
    1 teaspoon garlic, minced
    Juice of 2 lemons
    2 pounds fresh mushrooms, whole
    12 small potatoes, whole, peeled
    6 carrots, cut into 2-inch sections
    ½ cup cream
    2 tablespoons all-purpose flour
    Hot cooked rice

Sprinkle doves with salt and pepper and rub with butter. Place birds in a roasting pan, breast side down; add Worcestershire sauce, wine, thyme, parsley, garlic, and lemon juice. Bake in preheated oven at 350 degrees for 2 hours, basting every 15 minutes. Remove pan from oven and add mushrooms, potatoes, and carrots. Return to oven and bake for 1 hour longer. Remove birds and vegetables to warm platter; pour liquid from roaster into saucepan and add cream and flour. Cook over medium heat, stirring constantly, until gravy is thickened. Serve gravy over rice.

Serve this dish with crusty homemade bread and a salad with vinaigrette dressing.

❧ Potted Pigeon

    4 medium-sized pigeons, whole
    Salt
    Red pepper
    4 slices bacon, crumbled
    1 stalk celery, cut into ½-inch sections

1 teaspoon dried thyme
1 teaspoon garlic, minced
1 teaspoon fresh parsley, finely minced
½ teaspoon rubbed sage
1½ pints chicken stock

Clean and truss pigeons as for roasting. Salt and pepper thoroughly.

Sauté bacon in a skillet until crisp; remove bacon and set aside. Brown birds in bacon drippings, then place them in a baking dish or casserole; add bacon, celery, seasoning, and stock. Cover and bake in preheated oven at 350 degrees for 2 hours. Pigeons are done when they can be pierced easily with a two-tined fork.

Serve with poke sallet, home fries, and corn pone.

Mountain Laurel Squab

6 squabs
Salt
Red pepper
Butter or margarine, melted
2 cups chicken stock
1 bunch asparagus, cooked
5 small onions, boiled
1 cup potatoes, boiled
1 cup diced turnips, boiled
½ teaspoon dried thyme
1 teaspoon fresh parsley, finely minced
½ teaspoon garlic, minced

Clean and truss squabs. Sprinkle birds with salt and pepper. Brush with melted butter and place squabs in baking dish or casserole. Cover and bake in preheated oven at 350 degrees for 10 minutes. Add stock, cover, and bake at 300 degrees for 1½ hours. Remove squabs from oven and add vegetables and seasonings; return to oven for 20 minutes longer or until vegetables are thoroughly heated.

Serve with green salad and hot bread.

❧ Sherried Ptarmigan with Pecan Dressing

- 6 ptarmigan, 1 to 1¼ pounds each
- Salt
- Freshly ground black pepper
- 1 cup sherry
- ¼ cup apricot brandy
- ¾ cup butter or margarine, melted
- 1 cup bread crumbs
- ¾ cup pecans, chopped
- ¼ cup apricot brandy

Sprinkle ptarmigan cavities with salt and pepper. Secure neck skin to backs of birds with toothpicks; lift wing tips up and over backs so they are tucked under.

To prepare dressing, combine sherry, brandy, and ¼ cup butter in a large saucepan; cook over medium heat for 1 minute. Add bread crumbs and pecans, stirring lightly.

Lightly stuff cavities of ptarmigan with pecan dressing; close cavities and secure with toothpicks. Tie leg ends to tail with heavy string. Brush ptarmigan with butter. Combine remaining butter with brandy. Place birds, breast side up, in a large, shallow roasting pan. Bake birds in preheated oven at 350 degrees for 1 to 1½ hours, or until juices run clear when birds are pierced with a two-tined fork. Baste every 10 minutes with brandy mixture.

Serve with rutabaga au gratin, field peas, and sourdough bread.

❧ Ptarmigan with Orange Glaze

- ½ teaspoon basil
- ½ teaspoon tarragon
- ½ teaspoon thyme
- ½ teaspoon savory
- 4 ptarmigan, 1 to 1¼ pounds each
- ½ teaspoon salt
- ½ teaspoon freshly ground black pepper
- ¼ cup butter or margarine, melted
- ¼ cup orange marmalade
- Watercress
- Orange slices, peeled
- Lemon slices, peeled

Combine herbs and mix well. Sprinkle inside cavities of ptarmigan with herbs. Sprinkle birds with salt and pepper; brush skin of each with butter. Truss ptarmigan and place breast side up on a rack in a shallow roasting pan. Pour enough water into pan to cover bottom (about ¼ inch deep).

Place birds in upper half of oven and bake at 325 degrees for 45 minutes. Brush birds with butter and spoon 1 tablespoon marmalade onto each breast. Bake for an additional 30 to 45 minutes or until juice runs clear when thigh is pierced with a two-tined fork.

Remove birds from oven and place on warm platter; garnish with watercress, orange slices, and lemon slices.

Serve with baked yams and corn bread muffins.

Almond-Stuffed Woodcock

- 6 woodcock, 2½ to 3 pounds
- Salt
- Red pepper
- ½ cup onion, chopped
- 1 clove garlic, finely minced
- ½ cup toasted almonds, coarsely chopped
- ½ teaspoon salt
- ½ teaspoon thyme
- ½ teaspoon freshly ground black pepper
- ½ cup parsley, finely chopped
- 1 cup rice, cooked
- 3 tablespoons butter or margarine, melted
- ½ cup dry white wine

Wash woodcock with cold water and wipe dry; sprinkle inside and out with salt and pepper.

Sauté onions and garlic in a saucepan over medium heat until onions are transparent; stir in almonds, salt, thyme, pepper, parsley, and rice.

Stuff birds' cavities with almond dressing; sew up cavities or use toothpicks. Pour butter and wine over birds. Place on rack in roasting pan and bake, uncovered, at 400 degrees until browned. Reduce heat to 350 degrees, cover, and roast about 1 hour, or until birds are tender, basting often with butter, wine, and pan drippings.

Serve with glazed turnips, a green salad, and hot rolls.

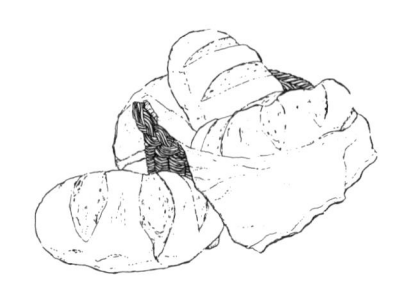

Braised Woodcock

8 tablespoons butter or margarine, melted
1 whole stalk celery, very thinly sliced
1 medium onion, thinly sliced
2 cloves garlic, finely chopped
½ teaspoon dried rosemary, crushed
½ teaspoon dried thyme, crushed
3 tablespoons vegetable oil
9 woodcock, whole, about 4 pounds
1 teaspoon salt
¼ teaspoon freshly ground black pepper
1 cup dry white wine
2 to 3 cups chicken stock

Preheat oven to 375 degrees.

Melt half the butter over medium-low heat in a heavy skillet. Add next 5 ingredients to hot butter. Sauté, stirring occasionally, for 15 to 20 minutes without browning. Set aside.

Pour oil into a large skillet and place over medium heat. Pat birds dry. Brown birds on all sides in hot oil.

Place birds in a baking pan, breast side up, and pour butter and sautéed vegetables from skillet over birds. Sprinkle with salt and pepper. Melt remaining butter and pour over birds. Add wine and enough stock to come about a third of the way up the side of birds.

Place birds in the oven and braise for 30 minutes, basting frequently with pan liquids.

Serve with boiled potatoes.

✎ Barbecued Sage Grouse

- 1 teaspoon garlic, finely minced
- ½ cup water
- ½ cup dry red wine
- ½ cup stock
- ½ cup vegetable oil
- ½ teaspoon salt
- ½ teaspoon freshly ground black pepper
- ½ teaspoon cayenne
- ½ tablespoon prepared mustard
- 1 tablespoon fresh lemon juice
- 2 tablespoons brown sugar
- 1 teaspoon onion juice
- ¼ cup tomato sauce
- 1 teaspoon chili powder
- 1 sage grouse, 5 to 6 pounds, cut into pieces

Combine all ingredients, except grouse, in blender and blend well. Pour into a saucepan and simmer over low heat for 1 hour, stirring occasionally.

Arrange grouse pieces, skin side up, on a lightly greased grill, about 4 inches from hot coals. Baste with barbecue sauce before and frequently during entire cooking time. Cook for 45 to 55 minutes, or until meat is no longer pink near bone.

✎ Breast of Grouse

- 4 ruffed grouse breasts, halved and boned
- Salt and pepper
- 3 tablespoons butter

    Remainder of 1 grouse (after breast is removed), cut up
 3 cups water
 2 small onions, finely chopped
 1 tablespoon parsley, finely chopped
 3 carrots, sliced into 1-inch sections
 1 stalk celery, cut into 1-inch sections
 1 bay leaf, crumbled
 1 cup stock
 3 tablespoons butter
 4½ tablespoons all-purpose flour
 ½ cup stewed tomatoes, strained
 ½ teaspoon salt
 ½ teaspoon garlic, minced
 2 tablespoons fresh lemon juice
 1 tablespoon fresh parsley, finely chopped
 1 pound fresh mushrooms, sliced and sautéed
 ½ teaspoon thyme
    Hot cooked rice
    Spiced apple rings

Sprinkle breasts with salt and pepper. Sauté in hot butter, uncovered, on one side for about 5 minutes or until browned. Turn breasts. Cover skillet; cook for another 5 minutes or until second side is browned; uncover and turn again. Cook for 5 minutes or until pieces are crisp. Remove pieces and set aside on a warm platter.

Place cut-up pieces of 1 grouse in saucepan; add water, onion, parsley, carrots, celery, and bay leaf and cook until stock is reduced to 1 cup.

To make sauce, place stock in a saucepan and add remaining ingredients. Place over medium heat and stir until sauce thickens and bubbles.

Serve breasts on mound of rice with sauce ladled over top. Garnish with spiced apple rings.

Grouse with Almond and Wine Sauce

- 4 ruffed grouse, 1 to 2 pounds each
- Salt
- Red pepper
- Butter
- 4 tablespoons butter or margarine
- Juice of 1 lemon
- ½ cup dry white wine
- 1 cup water
- ½ teaspoon thyme
- ½ teaspoon garlic, minced
- ¼ cup fresh parsley, chopped
- ½ cup almonds, coarsely chopped
- Salt and pepper

Sprinkle grouse with salt and pepper and rub inside and out with butter; bake in preheated oven at 350 degrees for 1½ hours, or until juices run clear when thigh is pierced with a two-tined fork, basting with a mixture of butter, lemon juice, and wine. Remove birds to warm plate.

Place roasting pan on top of stove, add water, thyme, garlic, and parsley, and bring to a boil.

Lightly brown almonds in butter in a skillet. Strain sauce from roasting pan into skillet. Season with salt and pepper to taste and pour over birds.

Serve with sautéed mushrooms, baked potatoes, green salad, hot biscuits, and cranberry jelly.

Woodbine Roast Partridge

- 6 partridge, about 1¼ pounds each
- Salt
- Red pepper
- Butter
- 1 teaspoon thyme
- 6 bay leaves
- 6 slices smoked bacon
- 3 teaspoons flour
- ½ cup dry white wine
- Juice of 1 lemon
- 4 tablespoons butter or margarine
- 3 tablespoons parsley, finely chopped

Sprinkle partridge with salt and pepper inside and out and rub with butter. Place a pinch thyme and 1 bay leaf in each bird's cavity. Place 1 strip bacon across each breast and fasten with toothpicks. Sprinkle ½ teaspoon flour over each bird.

Place partridge in roasting pan and bake in preheated oven at 350 degrees for about 1½ hours, basting occasionally with mixture of wine, lemon juice, and butter. When birds are done, sprinkle with parsley.

Serve with stuffed artichokes, braised okra, and snap bean salad.

Stuffing for Game Birds

❧ SAUSAGE STUFFING

- ½ pound sausage
- ½ cup onion, finely chopped
- 3 tablespoons fresh parsley, finely chopped
- ½ cup celery, finely chopped
- ¼ cup butter or margarine, melted
- ½ teaspoon thyme
- ½ teaspoon garlic powder
- 1 teaspoon salt
- ¼ teaspoon pepper
- 1 teaspoon poultry seasoning

Sauté sausage and drain off fat. Sauté onion, parsley, and celery in separate saucepan until onion is clear. Combine cooked ingredients and remaining ingredients in a mixing bowl; toss together lightly.

Makes about 2 cups, enough for 1 sage grouse, 1 small goose, 2 pheasants, or 1 large blue grouse.

❧ CHESTNUT AND CURRANT STUFFING

- 1 cup currants
- ½ cup boiling water
- 1 tablespoon sugar

Rind of 1 orange, grated
1 pound chestnuts
½ cup sherry
½ cup chicken broth
2½ cups bread crumbs
¼ cup parsley, finely chopped
¼ cup celery, chopped
¼ cup butter or margarine, melted
½ teaspoon salt
3 tablespoons apples, chopped

Cover currants with boiling water and let stand for 1 hour, then drain. Add sugar and orange rind to currants.

Boil chestnuts in a pot of boiling water for 3 minutes. Drain and peel. Combine chestnuts, sherry, and broth in a saucepan, and simmer for 20 minutes or until tender.

Combine currant and chestnut mixtures and remaining ingredients, tossing lightly. If too dry, add broth for desired consistency.

Makes about 5½ cups, enough to stuff 1 large Canada goose, 1 sage grouse, or 2 blue grouse.

RICE-RAISIN-ALMOND STUFFING

2 cups white rice, cooked
3 tablespoons white raisins
1 cup celery, chopped
¼ cup almonds, chopped
2 tablespoons butter or margarine, melted
1 tablespoon parsley, finely chopped
⅛ teaspoon pepper
2 teaspoons Worcestershire sauce
½ teaspoon salt

Combine all ingredients, mixing thoroughly.

Makes about 4 cups, enough to stuff 4 to 6 woodcock, bobwhite quail, or California quail.

❧ Corn Bread Stuffing

- 2 green onions with tops, chopped
- ½ cup celery, chopped
- ½ teaspoon garlic, minced
- 2 tablespoons parsley, finely chopped
- 4 cups stale corn bread
- 1 cup coarse dry bread crumbs
- ¼ cup butter or margarine, melted
- 1 cup boiling chicken broth
- 1 egg, beaten
- ½ teaspoon salt
- ⅛ teaspoon freshly ground black pepper
- ¼ teaspoon thyme
- ½ teaspoon sage

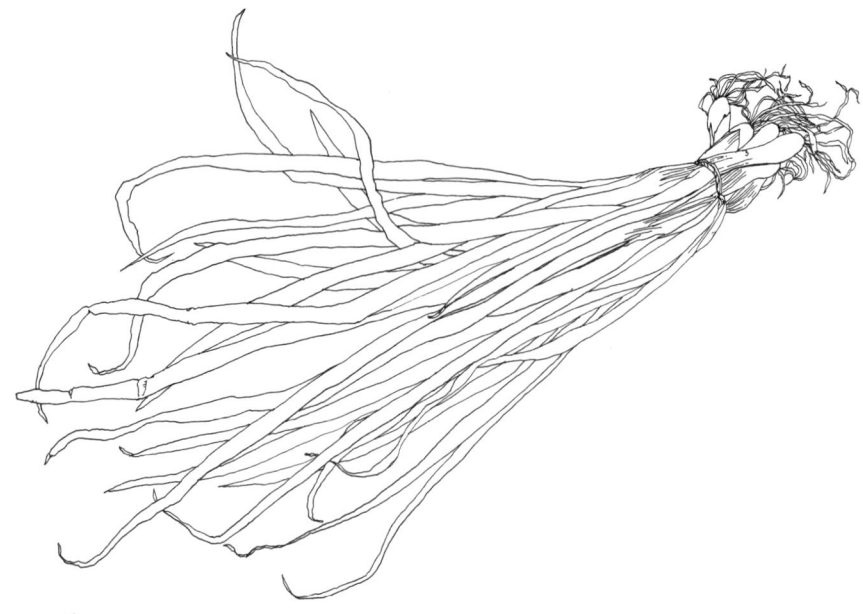

Sauté onion, celery, garlic, and parsley until onion is clear. Crumble corn bread in a large bowl; add dry bread crumbs and pour melted butter and broth over corn bread mixture; let stand for 15 minutes. Add sautéed onion mixture and remaining ingredients, mixing well. If mixture is too dry, add more broth to obtain desired consistency.

Makes about 6 cups, enough to stuff 1 large Canada goose, 1 sage grouse, or 8 to 10 mountain quail.

Bread Stuffing

- ¼ cup onion, finely chopped
- ½ cup butter or margarine, melted
- 1 teaspoon poultry seasoning
- ½ cup celery, finely chopped
- ¼ cup parsley, finely chopped
- 6 cups stale bread crumbs
- ¼ teaspoon garlic, minced
- ¼ teaspoon thyme
- ½ teaspoon sage
- ½ teaspoon salt
- ¼ teaspoon pepper
- ½ cup chicken stock

Sauté onions in butter until clear; remove from heat and set aside. Mix rest of ingredients, except stock, in a large bowl. Toss together; pour in stock and onion in butter. Mix thoroughly. Vary amount of stock to get desired consistency.

Makes about 7 cups, enough to stuff 1 large Canada goose, 1 turkey, or 4 to 6 sharp-tailed grouse.

FISH AND SHELLFISH

Fish and Shellfish

In general, fish fillets can be interchanged but fat-fleshed fish should be substituted for fat-fleshed fish, and lean-fleshed fish for lean-fleshed fish.

Cheesy Trout Deluxe

 3 pounds trout fillets
 1 teaspoon salt
 ½ teaspoon pepper
 1 tablespoon all-purpose flour
  Vegetable oil
 ½ cup onion, chopped
 ½ cup celery, chopped
 1 cup tomatoes, chopped
 ½ teaspoon garlic, minced
 ¼ teaspoon thyme
 ¼ teaspoon cayenne
  Juice of 1 lemon
 ½ cup dry white wine
 ½ cup mild cheddar cheese, diced
 1 tablespoon coriander or parsley, finely chopped

Rinse fillets and dry thoroughly with paper towels; cut into serving-sized pieces. Combine salt, pepper, and flour and dredge fillets in mixture.

 Heat vegetable oil in a large skillet; brown fillets quickly on both sides. Remove skillet from heat and drain excess oil. Add next 8 ingredients to fish. Continue cooking until vegetables are tender. Serve topped with cheese and sprinkled with coriander or parsley.

❧ Baked Trout in Wine Sauce

    1 cup dry white wine
  ¼ cup onion, chopped
     Juice of 1 lemon
  ¼ teaspoon paprika
1½ teaspoons salt
    2 teaspoons parsley, finely chopped
    2 tablespoons olive oil
    3 tablespoons butter or margarine, melted
  ¼ teaspoon dried thyme leaves
    3 pounds trout fillets, cut into serving-sized pieces
     Slivered almonds

Combine first 9 ingredients, mixing well. Preheat oven to 350 degrees.

Arrange fillets in a 3-inch-deep baking pan in a single layer. Pour mixture over fillets. Bake for 20 to 30 minutes, or until fish flakes easily when pricked with a fork. Garnish with slivered almonds.

❧ Herb-Stuffed Salmon

    6 pounds salmon, whole, cleaned and eyes removed
     Salt
     Freshly ground black pepper
    4 tablespooons butter or margarine
    4 green onions, including tops, chopped
  ½ teaspoon garlic, minced
  ½ cup dry white wine
     Juice of 1 lemon
1½ teaspoons parsley, finely chopped
  ¼ teaspoon thyme
  ¼ teaspoon oregano

¼ teaspoon marjoram
1½ cups dry bread crumbs
¼ teaspoon cinnamon
1 large onion, sliced
1 large lemon, sliced
2 cups stewed tomatoes, chopped

Sprinkle fish inside and out with salt and pepper.

Melt 2 tablespoons of butter in a saucepan and sauté onions and garlic until onions wilt. Add wine, lemon juice, parsley, thyme, oregano, and marjoram. Bring to a boil, remove from heat, and stir in bread crumbs.

Stuff salmon with bread crumb mixture and skewer the opening. Place fish in a baking pan or dish 2 inches deep; dot with remaining 2 tablespoons of butter. Sprinkle with cinnamon and arrange onion and lemon slices on top. Pour tomatoes around the sides of the fish.

Bake in a 425-degree oven for 25 minutes or until fish flakes easily when pricked with a fork.

Baked Salmon

    3 tablespoons butter or margarine
    ¼ cup olive oil
    ½ cup onions, finely chopped
    ½ cup all-purpose flour
    1 tablespoon garlic, finely minced
    ½ teaspoon dried thyme
    2 tablespoons fresh parsley, finely chopped
    ½ cup sweet green pepper, chopped
    ½ cup shallots, chopped
    ½ cup dry white wine
    ½ cup water
    ½ teaspoon freshly ground black pepper
  1½ teaspoons salt
    2 bay leaves
      Juice of 1 lemon
    ½ teaspoon dried basil
    2 pounds salmon steaks
    2 lemons, sliced

Preheat the oven to 375 degrees.

Melt butter in a saucepan over low heat; mix in olive oil. Add onions and sauté until tender, then stir in flour and brown. Add garlic, thyme, parsley, green pepper, and shallots and cook until the vegetables wilt. Add the next 7 ingredients and mix well.

Place salmon steaks in a 3-inch-deep baking dish and cover with sauce and lemon slices. Bake for 25 to 30 minutes. Fish is done when it flakes easily when pricked with a fork.

Melanie Suzanne's Stuffed Salmon

    3 tablespoons butter or margarine
    ½ cup young green onions, including tops, chopped
    ½ cup sweet green bell pepper, chopped
    3 tablespoons parsley, finely chopped
    ½ teaspoon garlic, finely minced

3 slices white bread, soaked in dry white wine and squeezed out
½ cup fresh mushrooms, thinly sliced
½ teaspoon salt
¼ teaspoon freshly ground black pepper
½ cup mild cheddar cheese
2 slices salmon steak, about 2 pounds
½ cup heavy cream
Paprika
¼ cup slivered almonds

Preheat the oven to 375 degrees.

Melt butter in a saucepan over medium heat and sauté onion, pepper, parsley, and garlic until tender. Remove from heat and mix in bread, mushrooms, salt, pepper, and cheese.

Butter an ovenproof dish, place 1 salmon slice in dish, and spread saucepan mixture over the top. Cover with the other salmon slice. Pour heavy cream over slices. Sprinkle with paprika and place almonds evenly on the top. Bake for 25 to 30 minutes.

Boiled Salmon with Tart Sauce

2 quarts water
2 pounds salmon, cut into 3-inch squares

Place water in pot and bring to a boil; add fish and bring to a boil again. Turn off heat and let fish stand in hot water for 20 minutes. Drain; serve with sauce spooned over top.

Tart Sauce

⅛ cup peanut oil
½ teaspoon salt
1 tablespoon fresh lemon juice
½ cup malt vinegar
¼ teaspoon freshly ground black pepper
1 tablespoon soy sauce

Blend all ingredients until smooth.

Crispy Lake Bass

½ cup yellow cornmeal
½ cup all-purpose flour
1 cup milk
1 egg, beaten
1 teaspoon baking powder
½ teaspoon salt
½ teaspoon dill weed
1 pound bass or other fish fillets, cut into serving-sized pieces

To make batter, combine all ingredients, except fish; mix well. Dip fish into batter, coating thoroughly. Fry in ½-inch-deep hot oil (375 degrees) for about 2 minutes per side or until crisp and golden brown, turning once. Drain on paper towels.
Serve with french fries and a colorful mixed salad.

Wine-Baked Striped Bass Fillets

¼ cup butter or margarine
¼ cup olive oil
½ cup onion, chopped
1 teaspoon garlic, finely minced
2 tablespoons parsley, finely minced
1 stalk celery, cut into 2-inch sections
2 cups tomatoes, chopped
3 bay leaves, crumbled
½ teaspoon thyme
½ teaspoon dried basil
Juice of 1 lemon
1 tablespoon salt
½ teaspoon freshly ground black pepper

½ cup dry white wine
3 pounds striped bass fillets

Melt butter in a 2-quart saucepan; mix in olive oil and sauté onion, garlic, parsley, and celery until tender. Remove pan from heat and stir in tomatoes, bay leaves, thyme, basil, lemon juice, salt, and pepper. Mix thoroughly; stir in wine.

Preheat the oven to 350 degrees.

Arrange fillets in a 3-inch-deep baking pan in a single layer. Pour contents of saucepan over fish. Bake for 20 to 30 minutes. Water may be added to sauce if necessary. When it is done, fish will flake easily when pricked with a fork.

Beer-Fried Bass

2 pounds bass fillets
1 cup flour
1 cup beer
1 egg, beaten
1 teaspoon salt
1 teaspoon baking powder
Vegetable oil for deep frying

Rinse fillets and place on paper towels to drain. Combine remaining ingredients, except oil, and mix thoroughly with a wire whisk or spoon. Preheat oil to 375 degrees in a deep fryer. Oil should be 1¾ to 3 inches deep.

Coat fillets by dipping them in batter mixture.

To fry, lower one to two fillets at a time into hot oil with tongs. Fry until golden brown — about 8 minutes. Drain fillets on paper towels.

Serve sprinkled with fresh lemon juice and paprika and garnish with lemon slices. Sautéed potatoes and sautéed onion rings go well with this dish.

SAVORY BAKED STRIPED BASS WITH PIQUANT SAUCE

4 pounds striped bass fillets
4 tablespoons butter or margarine, melted
½ cup dry white wine
1½ teaspoons salt
½ teaspoon cayenne
1 pound fresh mushroom caps, whole
½ cups onions, finely chopped
¼ teaspoon cumin
½ teaspoon thyme
Water

Preheat the oven to 350 degrees.
Place individual fillets in greased baking dish in a single layer. Brush with butter and add remaining ingredients. Add only enough water necessary for basting.
Basting every 5 minutes, bake for 20 to 30 minutes, depending on thickness of fillets, or until fish flakes easily when pricked with a fork.
Serve with Piquant Sauce.

Piquant Sauce

2 tablespoons butter or margarine
¼ cup onion, finely chopped
2 tablespoons all-purpose flour
1 cup fish stock
1 teaspoon vinegar
1 teaspoon parsley, chopped
1 teaspoon prepared mustard
1 teaspoon pickle relish
Salt and pepper to taste

Melt butter in a saucepan, add onion, and sauté until golden brown; then stir in flour and brown. Add stock slowly and stir until boiling. Reduce heat, add remaining ingredients, and simmer for 5 minutes.

Serve fillets with sauce.

✿ Baked Bluegill

    4 pounds bluegill, whole, with eyes removed
    1 tablespoon salt
    1 cup milk
    1 cup bread crumbs, finely sifted
      Butter or margarine
      Fresh lemon juice

Rinse bluegill and pat dry. Add salt to milk and mix well. Dip fish in milk, then in bread crumbs.

Place fish in a well-buttered baking pan and dot with butter. Brown fish in a 550-degree oven for about 10 to 20 minutes.

Serve with melted butter and lemon juice.

🌿 FISH AND CHIPS

    1½ pounds flounder fillets, cut into serving-sized pieces
    Salt and pepper
    ¾ cup flour, sifted
    ¾ teaspoon salt
    1 egg, slightly beaten
    ½ cup milk
    1 tablespoon butter or margarine, melted
    Vegetable oil for frying
    1½ pounds potatoes
    Tarragon or dill vinegar

Wash fish in salted water; dry on paper towels. Sprinkle with salt and pepper. Sift flour with salt. Combine egg, milk, and butter. Add to flour mixture and beat with a wire whisk until smooth.

    Preheat oil to 375 degrees in a deep fryer. Oil should be 1¾ to 3 inches deep.

    Peel and wash potatoes and cut each into 6 to 8 lengthwise sections. Fry in hot oil until golden brown. Drain on paper towels. Sprinkle lightly with salt; keep warm in 200-degree oven.

    Dip fish in flour batter and fry in same oil until brown. Drain on paper towels.

    Serve with mayonnaise, tartar sauce, or tomato catsup.

Mayonnaise

    1 egg yolk
    1 cup vegetable oil
    4 tablespoons fresh lemon juice or vinegar
    ½ teaspoon salt
    ¼ teaspoon white pepper

Beat egg yolk lightly in a bowl; add oil very slowly, beating con-

stantly. Add lemon juice slowly, continuing the beating process. Beat in salt and pepper.
Store mayonnaise in the refrigerator.

Tartar Sauce

    1 cup mayonnaise
    1 teaspoon prepared mustard
    1 teaspoon fresh parsley, finely chopped
    1 teaspoon capers, finely chopped
    1 teaspoon pickles, finely chopped
    ½ teaspoon onion juice

Add all ingredients to mayonnaise in the order given; stir well. Chill for several hours before serving.

Tomato Catsup

    4 quarts stewed tomatoes, chopped
    8 sweet green peppers, chopped
    4 tablespoons salt
    1 quart vinegar
    2 tablespoons white pepper
    3 tablespoons prepared mustard
    1 tablespoon allspice

Cook tomatoes, pepper, salt, and vinegar in a 6-quart pot until tender. Rub through a sieve, passing all the pulp possible; add remaining ingredients and bring to a boil. Reduce heat and simmer for three hours. Bottle and seal when cold.

Almond-Baked Fish Fillets

2 pounds haddock fillets
½ cup mayonnaise
Bread crumbs
½ teaspoon salt
¼ teaspoon black pepper, freshly ground
Fresh lemon juice
Almond halves, blanched

Brush fillets lightly with mayonnaise; then coat well with dry bread crumbs. Sprinkle both sides with salt and pepper.
Place fillets in a single layer in a well-greased shallow baking pan or dish. Arrange almond halves on top and sprinkle lightly with lemon juice.
Bake at 350 degrees for 15 minutes or until fish flakes easily when pricked with a fork.

Poached Fish Fillets

2 pounds fillets of sole, perch, or haddock
¼ cup dry white wine
½ teaspoon salt
¼ teaspoon freshly ground black pepper
Juice of 1 lemon
½ cup butter or margarine, melted
1 teaspoon dried dill
Cashew nuts
Lemon slices
Fresh parsley sprigs

Place fillets in a large skillet with straight sides; add wine, salt, pepper, lemon juice, and butter. Place the skillet over medium heat, cover, and poach for 10 minutes or until fish flakes easily when pricked with a fork.

Serve with sauce spooned over fillets and sprinkle with dill. Garnish with cashews, lemon slices, and parsley.

Stuffed Walleyed Pike

  1 large pike
1½ cups bread crumbs
  ½ cup milk
  2 tablespoons butter or margarine
  1 small onion, finely minced
  1 tablespoon parsley, finely chopped
  1 small egg, beaten
  Salt and pepper

Soak bread crumbs in milk briefly. Squeeze out excess milk and add butter, onion, parsley, egg, and seasonings to bread crumbs.

Fill pike with stuffing. Place on well-buttered aluminum foil. Wrap foil around pike, tightly securing ends to prevent juices from leaking out. Place on a baking sheet and bake at 350 degrees for 20 to 30 minutes, depending on size of fish.

Before serving, remove foil and sprinkle fish with lemon juice. Garnish with lemon slices and parsley sprigs.

✤ Skipper's Baked Bluefish

    1 large bluefish, 5 to 6 pounds
    ⅓ cup butter or margarine
    10 drops onion juice
    1 tablespoon fresh lemon juice
    1 tablespoon parsley, finely chopped
    ½ teaspoon salt
    ¼ teaspoon freshly ground black pepper

Split bluefish down the back; wipe it well and lay in a well-greased baking pan or dish.

Melt butter in a saucepan and stir in remaining ingredients, mixing well. Pour mixture over fish.

Bake in a 350-degree oven for 20 to 30 minutes or until fish flakes easily when pricked with a fork.

✤ Spicy Baked King Mackerel

    2 to 3 pounds mackerel fillets
    ¼ teaspoon pepper
    ¼ teaspoon cayenne
    1½ teaspoons garlic salt
    Few leaves rosemary
    3 tablespoons parsley, finely chopped
    Juice of 1 lemon
    ½ cup butter, melted

Preheat oven to 350 degrees.

Arrange fillets in a baking pan in a single layer. Mix remaining ingredients. Pour mixture over fillets and bake for 20 to 30 minutes or until fish flakes easily when pricked with a fork.

Old Irish Fish Casserole

½ cup water
½ cup milk
6 medium potatoes, peeled and sliced ¼ inch thick
2 pounds fish fillets, cut into 4-inch pieces
1 large onion, cut into ¼-inch slices and separated into rings
1 teaspoon salt
¼ teaspoon freshly ground black pepper
¼ teaspoon cumin
¼ teaspoon rosemary
¼ teaspoon tarragon
¼ cup shallots, chopped
6 slices sugar-cured bacon, cut into halves
½ cup cashew nuts or peanuts, coarsely chopped
½ cup mild cheddar cheese, diced
¼ cup parsley, finely chopped

Grease a 12-by-10-by-2-inch baking dish or casserole; pour in water and milk. Layer one-third of potatoes, fish fillets, and onion rings in pan. Mix salt, pepper, cumin, rosemary, and tarragon. Sprinkle one-third of herb mixture, shallots, bacon, and nuts over fish. Repeat, alternating layers of fish and herbs. Place cheese on top and sprinkle with parsley.

Cover with aluminum foil and bake in preheated oven at 350 degrees for 30 minutes or until onion and potatoes are tender and fish flakes when pricked with a fork.

Crusty homemade bread with butter and a green salad are all this dish needs as accompaniment.

⚞ Cumberland Mountain Fried Crappie

   12 large crappie, head, tail, and fins removed
   ½ cup milk
    2 eggs, beaten
    2 cups yellow cornmeal
 1½ teaspoons salt
    1 teaspoon freshly ground black pepper
      Vegetable oil, enough for ⅛ inch or more deep in frying pan

Wash crappie in salted water and drain on paper towels.

Combine milk and eggs in a mixing bowl. Combine cornmeal, salt, and pepper in a second bowl. Dip fish into first bowl, then into second, coating well.

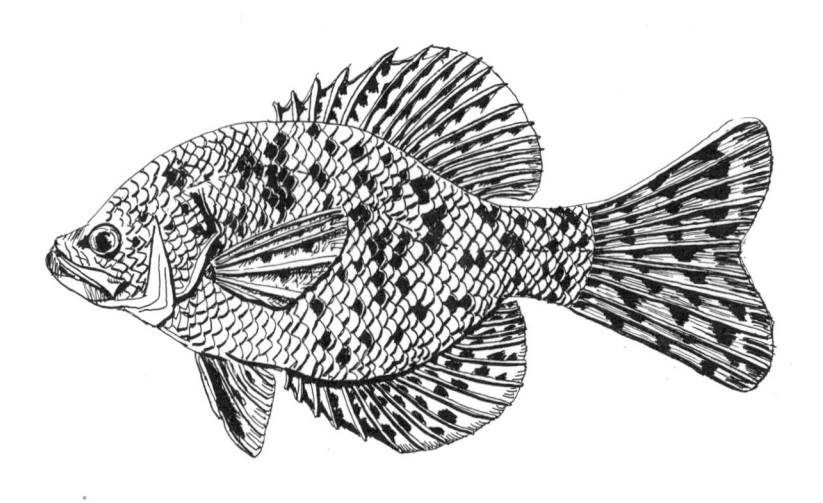

Heat vegetable oil in a heavy skillet. Fry fish, 2 at a time and not touching, for about 4 minutes on one side, then turn and fry for about 3 minutes on the other. Fish is done when it flakes easily when pricked with a fork. Drain on paper towels placed on a baking sheet. Keep warm in a 200-degree oven until all fish is fried and ready to serve.

Garnish with lemon slices and serve with tarragon or dill vinegar, or with your favorite sauce.

❧ Broiled Spicy Flounder

2 pounds flounder fillets
Butter or margarine, melted
½ cup catsup
¼ cup butter or margarine, melted
Juice of 1 lemon
2 tablespoons liquid smoke
½ teaspoon onion, grated
½ teaspoon dry mustard
½ teaspoon paprika
3 drops Tabasco sauce
¼ teaspoon thyme
1¼ teaspoon garlic salt

Cover broiler pan with foil; brush foil with butter. Arrange fish fillets on foil.

Combine remaining ingredients, mixing well. Brush mixture over fillets.

Broil about 4 inches from heat for 8 to 14 minutes or until fish flakes easily when pricked with a fork; baste once during broiling, but do not turn, because fillets may fall apart.

❧ Flounder with Wine Sauce

½ cup peanut oil
¼ cup green onions, chopped
½ teaspoon garlic, finely minced
2 teaspoons parsley, finely chopped
2 pounds flounder fillets
1 tablespoon all-purpose flour
1 bay leaf
½ teaspoon salt
¼ teaspoon freshly ground black pepper
⅛ teaspoon tarragon
 Pinch cinnamon
¼ cup dry white wine
 Lemon slices

Heat oil in a skillet over medium heat, add onion, garlic, and parsley, and sauté lightly. Add fillets and cook until browned on both sides, for about a total of 8 minutes; turn only once. Set fillets aside in skillet.

Place flour (blended with a little water), bay leaf, salt, pepper, tarragon, cinnamon, and wine in a saucepan; cook over medium heat until thickened, stirring constantly. Pour sauce over fillets and return the skillet to heat and simmer for 12 minutes. Garnish with lemon slices.

❧ Fried Catfish

12 pounds catfish fillets, sliced ⅛ inch thick
1 cup milk
2 eggs, beaten
1½ cups yellow cornmeal
2¼ teaspoons salt
1 teaspoon freshly ground black pepper
 Vegetable oil for frying

Rinse fillets and dry thoroughly with paper towels. Place fillets in a bowl and add milk and eggs to cover. Combine cornmeal and seasonings in a second bowl. Preheat 1¾ to 3 inches oil to 375 degrees in a deep fryer.

Remove fillets from first bowl, one at a time, allowing excess milk and egg to drop back into bowl, and place in second bowl, coating them in seasoned meal. Place fillets on a platter, not touching, to dry for about 5 minutes.

Fry until golden brown, for about a total of 5 to 7 minutes; turn only once. Drain on a paper-towel-lined platter and place in a preheated 200-degree oven to keep warm until serving time.

Serve with tartar sauce or malt vinegar.

Baked Catfish

- 4 pounds catfish fillets
- 5 tablespoons butter or margarine
- ¾ cup dry white wine
- ½ teaspoon fresh lemon juice
- 2 slices onion
- 2 tablespoons all-purpose flour
- ½ cup water
- 2 tablespoons heavy cream
- 2 egg yolks
- Salt and freshly ground black pepper
- Fresh parsley, finely chopped

Put fillets in a well-buttered baking pan and dot with 3 tablespoons butter. Add wine, lemon juice, and onion; cover and bake for 10 minutes in 400-degree oven. Drain and reserve cooking liquid; remove fillets to serving dish.

Place remaining 2 tablespoons butter in a saucepan, add flour, then gradually the reserved liquid, water, cream, egg yolks, salt, and pepper. Simmer until sauce is thickened; do not boil. Strain sauce over fish and sprinkle with parsley.

Creamy Crayfish Casserole

10 slices sugar-cured bacon
6 tablespoons butter or margarine
½ cup onion, chopped
¼ cup sweet green pepper, chopped
¼ cup shallots, chopped
2 pounds crayfish
¼ cup extra dry vermouth
½ cup chicken stock
1 teaspoon salt
¼ teaspoon freshly ground black pepper
½ teaspoon thyme
2 eggs, beaten
1½ cups half-and-half
1½ cups soft bread crumbs
½ cup mild cheddar cheese, shredded
2 tablespoons butter or margarine, melted
¼ teaspoon paprika
½ cup cashew nuts, chopped

Sauté bacon in a large, heavy skillet until cooked and drain off fat. Add butter, onion, green pepper, and shallots; sauté until tender, stirring frequently. Stir in crayfish and cook, stirring constantly, for 1 minute. Stir in wine, stock, salt, pepper, thyme, and eggs. Simmer for 3 to 5 minutes. Stir in half-and-half, mixing well. Simmer until thickened. Pour into baking dish.

Combine bread crumbs, cheese, and butter; sprinkle over top of casserole. Bake, uncovered, in preheated oven at 350 degrees for 10 to 15 minutes or until cheese melts and dish is heated through. Garnish with paprika and cashews.

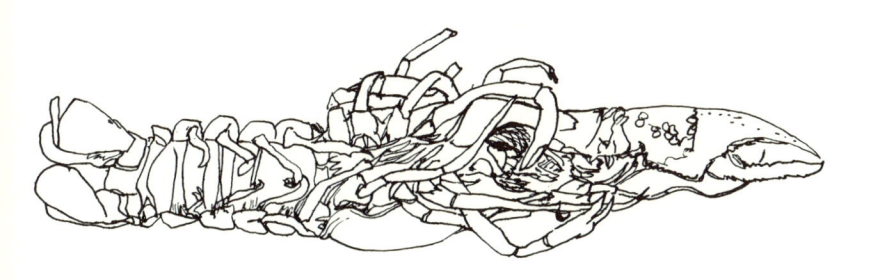

Old Kentucky Creamed Crayfish

- 2 tablespoons butter or margarine
- 1 tablespoon parsley, finely chopped
- 1 teaspoon onion, chopped
- 2 cups boiled crayfish
- ½ cup sherry or Madeira
- 1 cup rice, cooked
- ⅔ cup heavy cream
- ½ teaspoon salt
- Pinch cayenne
- ½ cup cashew nuts, chopped

Melt butter in a heavy skillet, add parsley and onion, then sauté over medium heat until onion is transparent. Reduce heat to low; add crayfish and sherry and simmer for 5 minutes. Stir in rice and cream. When thoroughly heated, add salt and cayenne. Garnish with cashews.

❧ Sherried Mussels and Crayfish with Brandy Sauce

- 2 cups fresh mushroom caps, halved
- 1 cup mussels
- ½ teaspoon salt
- 1 cup crayfish
- ½ cup sherry
- ½ cup butter or margarine

Sauce

- 2 tablespoons butter or margarine
- 1 tablespoon all-purpose flour
- ¾ cup heavy cream
- 2 egg yolks, slightly beaten
- 1 tablespoon brandy
- ½ cup cashew nuts, halved
- Pinch cayenne

Place mushrooms, mussels, salt, crayfish, and sherry in a stainless-steel or porcelain bowl and let stand for 1 hour.

Melt butter in skillet over medium heat, add mushrooms, mussels, and crayfish, and cook, covered, for 8 minutes, uncovering occasionally to turn. Set aside.

Melt butter in a saucepan over medium-low heat, add flour, and stir to form a smooth paste. Reduce heat slightly and cook for 4 to 5 minutes, stirring occasionally.

When paste is golden, slowly stir in cream, then egg yolks and brandy. Slowly bring sauce to a boil, stirring to prevent scorching. Once sauce comes to a complete boil and is fully thickened, pour it over mussels and crayfish. Simmer over low heat for 3 minutes.

Garnish with cashews. Sprinkle very lightly with cayenne.

Pan-Fried Mussels

2 eggs, beaten
2 tablespoons milk
1½ cups all-purpose flour
1½ cups dry bread crumbs
½ teaspoon salt
⅛ teaspoon freshly ground black pepper
2½ cups mussels
Vegetable oil

Combine eggs and milk in a small mixing bowl. Combine flour, bread crumbs, salt, and pepper in a plastic bag; mix well. Dip mussels, 1 at a time, in egg mixture, then place in bag of crumb mixture and shake, coating well. Sauté for 5 minutes in hot oil, carefully turning once. Drain on paper towels.
 Serve with catsup or your favorite sauce.

Deep-Fried Mussels

1½ pounds mussels, shelled and left whole
2 small eggs, slightly beaten
1 cup yellow cornmeal
Salt and freshly ground black pepper to taste

Preheat oil to 375 degrees in a deep fryer with a wire basket. Oil should be at least 3 inches deep.
 Drain mussels, dip in egg, then roll in cornmeal seasoned with salt and pepper. Drop at once into hot oil. Mussels should brown almost immediately. Do not fry too many at a time, to prevent their becoming soggy.

✯ Oven-Fried Mussels

 1 cup all-purpose flour
 1 teaspoon salt
 ¼ teaspoon pepper
 2 eggs, slightly beaten
 1 cup bread crumbs
 ½ cup olive or vegetable oil
 4 cups mussels, shelled and left whole

Place flour, salt, and pepper in a small bowl and mix well. Put eggs in a second small bowl and the bread crumbs in a third. Use a fourth bowl for oil. Using tongs to hold mussels, coat them in the first bowl, dip in the second, roll in the third, and dip in the fourth.

Arrange mussels in a shallow baking dish. Bake in preheated oven at 400 degrees for 15 minutes or until well browned.

✯ Mussel Fritters

  Vegetable oil, for frying
 1⅓ cups flour
  2 teaspoons baking powder
  ½ teaspoon salt
  ¼ teaspoon pepper
  2 eggs, slightly beaten
  ⅓ cup milk
  2 cups mussels, shelled and chopped

Preheat oil to 375 degrees in a deep fryer with a wire basket. Oil should be at least 3 inches deep and hot enough to brown a 1-inch cube of bread in 1 minute.

Place flour, baking powder, salt, and pepper in a bowl and mix well. Stir in eggs and milk and blend together. Add mussels and stir well until thoroughly coated with batter. Dip a metal tablespoon end into hot oil, then a spoonful of mussel mixture and drop it into oil carefully. Fry several at a time, being sure not to overcrowd them, for 3 to 5 minutes or until lightly browned. Remove with the wire basket and drain on paper towels.

Mussel Fricassee

2 tablespoons butter or margarine
2 cups mussels, shelled and chopped
2 tablespoons all-purpose flour
½ cup heavy cream
1 egg yolk, slightly beaten
½ teaspoon salt
¼ teaspoon pepper
  Hot cooked rice
  Cashew nuts

Melt butter in a skillet; add mussels and sauté over medium heat for 5 minutes. Add flour and lightly brown; gradually pour on cream and egg yolk, then cook for 3 minutes longer or until thickened. Season with salt and pepper.
Serve hot, ladled over rice. Sprinkle with cashews.

Mountain Mussel Soup

 2 tablespoons butter or margarine
24 mussels, shelled and chopped
 2 tablespoons all-purpose flour
4½ cups heavy cream
½ teaspoon salt
⅛ teaspoon freshly ground white pepper
 1 tablespoon parsley, finely chopped

Melt butter in a skillet over medium heat; add mussels and sauté for 3 minutes, turning occasionally. Remove mussels from skillet, draining excess butter back into the skillet, and set aside. Gradually add flour to the skillet, stirring constantly. Slowly stir in cream; bring to a boil. Add remaining ingredients and simmer for 5 minutes or until desired thickness is reached.

Clam Chowder

1 cup water
18 clams, finely chopped
3 potatoes, diced into ¼-inch pieces
2 slices bacon, cut into small pieces
1 cup onion, finely chopped
2 cups milk
2 cups light cream
2 tablespoons butter or margarine
2 tablespoons all-purpose flour
1 teaspoon parsley, finely chopped
1 teaspoon salt
Freshly ground black pepper to taste

Place water, clams, and potatoes in a 2-quart saucepan; cook over medium heat until potatoes are tender.

Fry bacon in a skillet until crisp; remove from drippings and add to saucepan. Sauté onions in drippings until they are clear; add onions to the saucepan, then milk, cream, and butter. Mix flour and a little water and add to the saucepan, along with parsley, salt, and pepper. Stir well and simmer over medium heat for 10 minutes or until soup is thickened and hot.

Frogs' Legs, Turtle, and Rattlesnake

Crispy Frogs' Legs

- 1 egg, beaten
- ½ cup milk
- Vegetable oil for frying
- ½ cup all-purpose flour
- ½ cup yellow cornmeal
- ½ teaspoon garlic, minced
- 1 teaspoon salt
- ¼ teaspoon freshly ground black pepper
- 12 pairs small frogs' legs

Combine egg and milk in a bowl. Preheat 1¾ to 3 inches oil to 375 degrees in a deep fryer. Combine flour, cornmeal, garlic, salt, and pepper in a second bowl. Dip frogs' legs in first bowl, then coat thoroughly in second bowl. Fry a few at a time in hot oil until golden brown — about 5 to 8 minutes.

Great at parties. Serve with crusty garlic bread.

Fancy Baked Frogs' Legs

½ cup butter or margarine, melted
¾ cup Parmesan cheese, grated
¾ to 1 teaspoon garlic, minced
½ teaspoon salt
16 frogs' legs
1 to 1½ cups soft bread crumbs

Combine butter, cheese, garlic, and salt; mix well. Dip each leg in mixture, then coat with bread crumbs. Place frogs' legs in a greased baking dish; spoon remaining butter mixture on top. Bake at 350 degrees for 1 hour or until tender.

Frogs' Legs and Sausage

½ pound sausage meat
12 frogs' legs
2 tablespoons butter or margarine, melted
½ cup dry red wine
1 pound fresh mushroom caps
1½ cups cream
1 tablespoon cornstarch
1 tablespoon cold water
1 egg yolk, slightly beaten
Salt and pepper to taste

Place sausage meat and frogs' legs in a skillet and fry for 5 minutes over medium heat. Remove skillet from heat, drain off fat, and add butter, wine, and mushroom caps; let stand for 30 minutes. Cover and cook over medium heat for 5 minutes. Set aside.

Scald cream in a double boiler. Mix cornstarch with cold water, add it gradually to cream, and simmer for 20 minutes, stirring constantly until mixture thickens. Stir in egg yolk.

Add cream mixture to sausage mixture in skillet. Reheat, season, and serve hot.

Turtle Fricassee with Wine

- 2½ to 3 pounds turtle meat
- Salt
- Red pepper
- Flour for dredging
- ½ cup dry white wine
- ¼ cup onion, chopped
- Juice of 1 lemon
- 1 teaspoon parsley, finely chopped
- 3 tablespoons butter or margarine
- ¼ teaspoon dried thyme leaves
- 1 teaspoon dried tarragon

Rinse turtle pieces and pat dry with paper towels. Sprinkle with salt and red pepper. Dredge in flour. Heat oil in a large skillet over medium heat. Brown pieces on all sides — about 10 minutes. Reduce heat to low. Drain off oil. Add remaining ingredients, cover, and continue to cook for about 45 minutes or until tender.

This fricassee, which is simple and honest in flavor, is delicious with boiled potatoes, a green salad, and a crusty, homemade bread.

⚜ Fried Succulent Snapper

1 snapping turtle, 5 to 10 pounds, cut into
  2- to 2½-inch sections
Salt
Red pepper
Flour for dredging
Vegetable oil

Soak skinned turtle meat in 1 gallon of water, 2 tablespoons baking soda, and 4 tablespoons of salt, and let stand in refrigerator overnight. Drain meat and pat dry with paper towels. Salt and pepper pieces and dredge in flour. Heat oil, ¼ inch deep, in a large skillet over medium heat.

Add turtle meat to the skillet and brown on one side for about 5 minutes, turn and brown on the other side for about 4 minutes, and turn again. Cover, reduce heat to low, and continue cooking for about 45 minutes or until meat is tender.

⚜ Camp Town Turtle Soup

1 snapping turtle, 10 to 12 pounds
Turtle broth
1½ cups cabbage, shredded
1 cup sweet whole-kernel corn
1 cup young sweet peas
1 cup dried navy beans
1 cup carrots, diced
½ cup celery, finely chopped
4 cups potatoes, diced
½ cup onions, chopped
1 quart tomato juice

½ cup green pepper, finely chopped
1 teaspoon freshly ground black pepper
1 tablespoon salt
½ teaspoon cayenne
½ teaspoon dried thyme leaves
  Water
3 tablespoons browned flour
1 cup noodles, uncooked
2 hard-boiled eggs, diced

Boil whole turtle until meat can be easily removed from its bones. Remove meat, discard bones, and save broth.

Place meat, broth, and next 14 ingredients in a 10-quart pot and cover with water. Simmer until vegetables wilt; then stir in flour, noodles, and eggs and continue cooking for another 15 minutes until vegetables are tender.

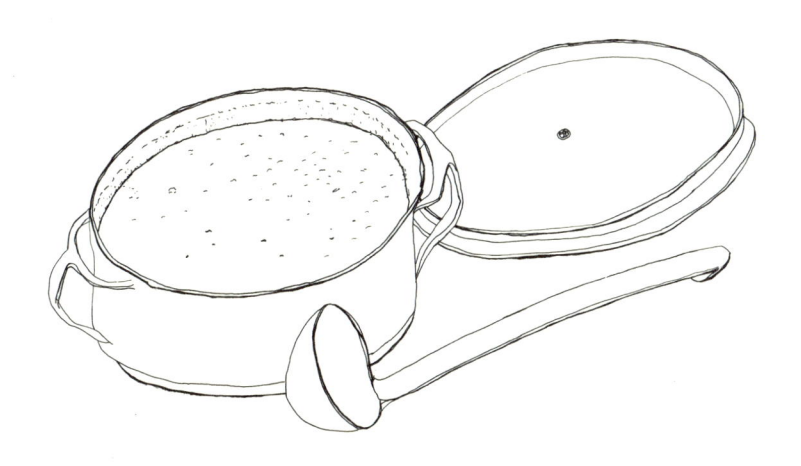

⚜ Tennessee Turtle Soup

   2 pounds turtle meat
      Water
   2 bay leaves
   2 cloves garlic, crushed
   6 cloves, whole
   3 tablespoons butter or margarine
   1 small onion, minced
   ½ cup all-purpose flour
2½ cups tomatoes, chopped
   1 cup sherry
   ¼ teaspoon cayenne
   ¼ teaspoon thyme
   ¼ teaspoon freshly ground black pepper
   1 sweet green bell pepper
   1 tablespoon Worcestershire sauce
   ½ teaspoon allspice
   1 teaspoon salt
   1 tablespoon parsley, finely chopped

Place turtle meat in a large pot, cover with water, add bay leaves, garlic, and cloves and cook for about 45 minutes or until meat is tender. Remove meat and mince it; set aside. Strain stock and set aside. Melt butter in the empty pot and add onion; sauté over medium heat until tender. Add flour, stirring constantly. When flour starts to brown, stir in stock gradually. Add turtle meat and stir in remaining ingredients; simmer for 30 minutes.

⚜ Cumberland Mountain Terrapin

½ cup all-purpose flour
¼ teaspoon paprika
½ teaspoon salt
¼ teaspoon pepper

½ cup butter or margarine
2½ to 3 pounds terrapin meat, deboned and cut into small pieces
½ cup sherry
1 teaspoon fresh lemon juice
1 tablespoon brandy
½ cup mushrooms, thinly sliced
1 tablespoon parsley, finely chopped
½ cup sour cream

Combine flour, paprika, salt, and pepper and mix well. Coat terrapin meat with mixture. Melt butter in a skillet, then brown terrapin meat on both sides. Combine sherry and lemon juice in a mixing bowl and pour over terrapin. Cover and simmer for 45 minutes; water may be added if necessary. Remove tender terrapin meat and set aside on a warm plate.

Add brandy, mushrooms, parsley, and sour cream to the skillet terrapin was cooked in; blend well and heat to desired thickness.

Serve terrapin with sauce ladled over the top.

❧ Kentucky Terrapin

    2 tablespoons butter or margarine
    2 tablespoons all-purpose flour
    1 cup light cream
    ¼ teaspoon allspice
    1 tablespoon sherry
      Pinch cayenne
    ½ cup fresh mushrooms, thinly sliced
    ¼ teaspoon freshly ground black pepper
    ½ teaspoon salt
    2½ to 3 pounds terrapin meat, deboned and cut into small pieces
    6 hard-boiled eggs, finely chopped
    ½ cup slivered almonds

Melt butter in a skillet, add flour, and brown lightly; then pour on cream while stirring slowly. Stir in allspice, sherry, cayenne, mushrooms, pepper, salt, and terrapin meat. Cook over medium heat for 1 hour or until meat is tender.

Serve over chopped eggs and top with almonds.

❧ Rattlesnake Fillets

    4 1¼- to 1½-inch-thick rattlesnake fillets
    4 tablespoons plus 1 teaspoon butter or margarine
    1 pound fresh mushrooms, sliced
    1 tablespoon shallot, minced
    ½ cup plus 2 tablespoons dry red wine
    1 teaspoon all-purpose flour
      Salt and pepper to taste
      Tomato wedges

Sauté fillets in 2 tablespoons butter for 5 minutes on each side or until tender; remove from skillet and keep warm. Drain and discard pan drippings. Melt 1 tablespoon butter in skillet over low heat; sauté mushrooms and shallots for 3 minutes. Stir in ½ cup wine; cook over low heat until wine is reduced to half.

Combine 1 teaspoon butter and flour to form a smooth paste; add to mushroom mixture. Cook, stirring constantly, for 30 seconds. Add remaining tablespoon butter and 2 tablespoons wine; stir until butter melts.

Serve sauce spooned over rattlesnake fillets. Garnish with tomato wedges.

Nice with sautéed potatoes, young green beans, and crusty homemade bread.

Savory Rattlesnake and Browned Duck Liver

½ pound rattlesnake meat, thinly sliced
½ pound duck liver, thinly sliced
   Salt and pepper
   Lemon slices
1 onion, thinly sliced
3 sprigs parsley

Sprinkle rattlesnake and liver with salt and pepper; let stand for 2 hours. Fry in deep fat (390 degrees) for 1 minute. Drain. Garnish with lemon and onion slices and parsley.

Serve with crackers as an hors d'oeuvre.

When you serve this dish at parties, you will earn a reputation as a gourmet cook. It's guaranteed to arouse your guests' interest, stimulate the conversation, and enhance your fame as a host.

Sautéed Rattlesnake Steaks

    4 tablespoons butter or margarine
    1 pound rattlesnake steaks
    Salt and pepper

Melt butter in a heavy skillet over medium-low heat. When butter is hot, add rattlesnake steaks and sauté for 8 to 10 minutes, turning frequently. Steaks should be watched carefully and turned as soon as they begin to get plump. Regulate the heat so that steaks develop a light, golden hue but never brown. When turning steaks, use tongs, not a fork, to avoid piercing the meat. Salt and pepper to taste.

Buttered green beans, peas, brussels sprouts, or broccoli go well with sautéed rattlesnake steaks, adding color and texture to the plate.

Flambéed Rattlesnake

    5 tablespoons butter or margarine
    1 cup rattlesnake meat, deboned and chopped
    ½ cup fresh mushrooms, chopped
    ½ teaspoon parsley, finely chopped
    ½ teaspoon salt
    ⅓ cup brandy
    6 ounces cream cheese
    ¼ teaspoon paprika
    ⅛ teaspoon garlic powder

Melt butter in a heavy skillet over medium-low heat. When butter is hot, add rattlesnake and sauté until tender. Add mushrooms, parsley, and salt. Cook for 5 minutes. Drain butter from skillet. Place skillet over heat again, add brandy, and ignite with a match. Let flame for a few seconds, then extinguish by placing lid on skillet. Blend in cheese, paprika, and garlic powder.

Spoon on crackers and serve as an hors d'oeuvre.

Rattlesnake Delight

    1 cup rattlesnake meat, deboned and chopped
    2 tablespoons butter or margarine
    ½ tablespoon onion, chopped
    ¼ teaspoon garlic, minced
    1 cup soft bread crumbs
    1 hard-boiled egg yolk
      Chicken stock or water
      Salt and pepper to taste
      Lettuce

Sauté chopped meat in butter in a saucepan over medium heat for 8 minutes. Add onion and garlic and cook until onion is clear. Remove from heat and add bread crumbs and egg yolk; mix well. Stir in enough stock or water to moisten. Add salt and pepper to taste.

    Wrap mixture in small, crisp lettuce leaves, allowing 2 tablespoons for each portion; fasten with toothpicks.

    Serve as an appetizer.

Rattlesnake Cocktail

    1 cup rattlesnake meat, cooked and chopped
    ½ cup catsup
    2 teaspoons Worcestershire sauce
    ½ teaspoon Tabasco sauce
      Juice of 1 lemon
    ¼ teaspoon salt
      Lettuce

Combine all ingredients, mixing well. Chill.

    Wrap mixture in small, crisp lettuce leaves, allowing 2 tablespoons for each portion. Fasten with toothpicks.

    Serve as an appetizer.

Favorite Accompaniments

❧ Old-Time Hardtack

Hundreds of years ago almost all cooks followed this recipe. Hardtack was used chiefly as an army ration and aboard ships. All early American settlers and frontiersmen carried hardtack in their saddlebags or packs. It was considered a hard biscuit rather than a cookie. Recipes may vary, but the original ingredients did not include salt.

3 eggs
1 cup sugar
1 cup flour
1 cup black walnuts, chopped
1 cup raisins or dates, chopped
1 teaspoon baking powder
1 teaspoon vanilla
Powdered sugar

Preheat the oven to 350 degrees.

Beat eggs and stir in sugar; add remaining ingredients and blend together. Grease shallow pan. Pour batter into pan and bake for 20 minutes. Cool; cut into sections and sprinkle with powdered sugar. Yield: 2 dozen.

Baking Powder Biscuits

    2 cups all-purpose flour
    ½ teaspoon salt
    4 teaspoons baking powder
    2 tablespoons shortening
    ¾ cup milk

Sift all dry ingredients in a medium-sized mixing bowl; cut in shortening as lightly as possible. Gradually add milk to make a very soft dough. Turn dough onto a well-floured board; knead lightly a few times. Roll dough to ¾ inch thickness. Cut with a floured biscuit cutter. Place on lightly greased baking sheet; bake at 425 degrees for 10 to 12 minutes. Yield: 12 to 18 biscuits.

Buttermilk Biscuits

    2 cups all-purpose flour, sifted
    ½ teaspoon salt
    ½ teaspoon baking soda
    3 teaspoons baking powder
    1 tablespoon shortening
    1 cup buttermilk

Combine all dry ingredients in a medium-sized mixing bowl; cut in shortening as lightly as possible. Stir in enough buttermilk to make a very soft dough. Turn dough onto a well-floured board; knead lightly a few times. Roll dough to ¾ inch thickness. Cut with a floured biscuit cutter. Place on a lightly greased baking sheet; bake at 425 degrees for 10 to 12 minutes. Yield: 12 to 18 biscuits.

Whole Wheat Biscuits

    2 cups whole wheat flour
    4 teaspoons baking powder
    ½ teaspoon salt
    2 tablespoons shortening
    1 small egg, beaten
    1 cup milk

Combine flour, baking powder, and salt; cut in shortening until mixture resembles coarse meal. Stir in egg and milk. Turn dough out onto a floured surface; roll to ½ inch thickness. Cut with a floured biscuit cutter. Place on a well-greased baking sheet and bake at 400 degrees for 12 to 15 minutes. Yield: 12 to 16 biscuits.

For rye biscuits, substitute rye flour.

Potato Biscuits

    1½ cups all-purpose flour
    4 teaspoons baking powder
    ½ teaspoon salt
    ¼ cup shortening
    1 cup milk
    1½ cups potatoes, cooked and mashed

Combine flour, baking powder, and salt; cut in shortening. Combine milk and potatoes, mixing well; add to flour mixture and stir well. Turn dough out onto a well-floured surface; knead lightly a few times. Roll to ½ inch thickness. Cut with a floured biscuit cutter. Place on a well-greased baking sheet and bake in preheated oven at 425 degrees for 12 to 15 minutes. Yield: 24 biscuits.

❧ CRACKLING BREAD

Americans have enjoyed crackling bread for over a hundred years; it is believed to have been invented by early black Americans in North Carolina. Cracklings or cracklins are browned bits of salt pork fried crisp.

- 2 cups buttermilk
- 2 cups yellow cornmeal
- 1 cup flour
- 1 teaspoon salt
- 1 teaspoon baking soda
- 1 egg
- 2 tablespoons shortening, melted
- 1 cup cracklings

Preheat the oven to 450 degrees.

Grease an 11-by-7-by-1½-inch baking pan. Combine all ingredients and mix well. Allow baking pan to heat in oven for a few minutes. Pour batter into hot, greased pan. Bake for 20 minutes. Let cool before slicing.

Serve with meals or as a snack with a tall glass of cold buttermilk.

❧ COUNTRY CORN BREAD

- 2 eggs, beaten
- 2 cups buttermilk
- 2 cups yellow cornmeal
- ½ teaspoon salt
- 1 teaspoon baking soda
- 2 teaspoons baking powder
- 3 tablespoons all-purpose flour
- 3 tablespoons sugar
- 2 tablespoons shortening, melted

Preheat the oven to 450 degrees.

Place a well-greased 10-inch iron skillet in oven. Combine eggs and buttermilk in a mixing bowl; stir in remaining ingredients and mix well. Pour batter into hot iron skillet. Bake for about 25 minutes or until browned.

❧ Pawpaw Muffins

Pawpaw is a delicious fruit that grows wild throughout the eastern half of the United States. American Indians and early settlers enjoyed it hundreds of years ago. The Indians claimed that this fruit healed stomach ulcers, but most people eat it just for its wonderful flavor. Pawpaw is half as long as a banana, which it closely resembles in taste and, unlike a banana, contains large seeds.

- 1½ cups flour
- ⅓ teaspoon salt
- 3 teaspoons baking powder
- 1 egg yolk
- ¼ cup shortening, melted
- ¼ cup milk
- 1 cup pawpaw, seeds and skin removed (bananas may be used)
- 1 egg white, stiffly beaten
- ¼ cup walnuts, chopped

Sift together flour, salt, and baking powder. Add egg yolk, shortening, and milk and beat well. Mix in pawpaw. Fold in egg white and nuts. Bake in greased muffin pans for 15 to 20 minutes in a preheated 400-degree oven.

❧ Jennifer's Hush Puppies

- 3 cups yellow cornmeal
- 1½ teaspoons salt
- 2 teaspoons baking powder
- 1 teaspoon baking soda
- ½ cup all-purpose flour
- 2 eggs, beaten
- 2 cups buttermilk
- ¼ cup onion, finely chopped
- ¼ cup crisp fried bacon, crumbled
- Vegetable oil for deep frying

Combine cornmeal, salt, baking powder, baking soda, and flour. Add eggs and buttermilk, mixing lightly. Stir in onion and bacon. Carefully drop batter by tablespoonfuls into deep, hot (370 degrees) oil. Fry until golden brown, turning once. Yield: 36 hush puppies.

Old-Time Corn Fritters

    2 cups cream-style corn
    2 eggs, separated
    2 tablespoons all-purpose flour
    ½ teaspoon salt
    ¼ teaspoon freshly ground black pepper
    3 tablespoons butter or margarine

Mix corn and egg yolks; blend in flour, salt, and pepper. Beat egg whites with a rotary mixer until soft peaks are formed. Fold into corn mixture until well blended. Melt butter in a heavy skillet, drop teaspoonfuls into hot butter, and brown for about 2 minutes on each side. Remove to warm platter and continue with the rest of the batter. Yield: 36 fritters.

Granny's Egg Bread

    2 cups white cornmeal
    1 teaspoon salt
    3 teaspoons baking powder
    3 eggs, beaten
    1 tablespoon shortening, melted
    1½ cups milk
    1 cup rice, cooked

Sift together cornmeal, salt, and baking powder; stir in eggs, shortening, milk, and rice. Beat thoroughly. Pour into a shallow, well-greased pan and bake in preheated oven at 425 degrees for 30 minutes.

❧ Home-Fried Potatoes

> 8 small potatoes, peeled and thinly sliced crossways
> 1 teaspoon salt
> ½ teaspoon freshly ground black pepper
> ½ teaspoon paprika
> ½ cup onion, finely chopped (optional)
> ⅓ cup vegetable oil or bacon drippings

Slice potatoes into circular pieces, about ¼ inch thick or a little thicker. Sprinkle with salt, pepper, and paprika. Heat vegetable oil in skillet over medium heat; add potatoes and onions. Fry until browned on both sides — about 5 minutes. Cover, reduce heat to low, and simmer for about 20 minutes, turning occasionally. Drain on paper towels.

❧ Poke Sallet

Poke is a green, leafy plant that grows wild throughout the Appalachian Mountains and other parts of the United States. It is prepared in a dish called poke sallet. Only the top tender leaves are picked for cooking, usually in the spring of the year. Cooked poke resembles cooked spinach. Some people claim poke has healing powers for the lower digestive system.

> 8 slices sugar-cured bacon
> 2 pounds poke
> 2 tablespoons vegetable oil
> 1 1-inch piece fresh ginger root, peeled and minced
> ½ teaspoon garlic, minced

Fry bacon until crisp, removing all fat; crumble and set aside.

Wash poke thoroughly and dry lightly. Put oil, ginger, and garlic in a large skillet and place over medium heat. When oil is heated, add poke and stir well, cover, and cook for 1 minute; toss lightly. Add crisp bacon and cook for 1 minute longer. Serve immediately.

❦ Fried Green Tomatoes

    6 small green tomatoes
    Salt and pepper to taste
    ½ teaspoon garlic, finely minced (optional)
    1 cup white cornmeal
    Vegetable oil or bacon drippings

Slice green tomatoes into ¼-inch slices. Season with salt, pepper, and garlic; dredge in cornmeal. Heat oil in skillet over medium-low heat; add green tomato slices and fry slowly until browned, turning once.

❦ Shuck Beans

Years ago, people preserved food in different ways, and today, some of those methods are still used. Green beans were placed in canning jars, but also dried whole. The taste of canned green beans and dried green beans is not the same. Dried green beans, called shuck beans, are strung on a threaded line and hung up in a hot, dry place to dry, and then stored for the winter. The flavor of shuck beans is distinctively different; once you have tried them you will agree that they are most delicious.

    2 pounds dried shuck beans
    ½ pound sugar-cured bacon, cut into 1-inch lengths
    2 teaspoons salt

Rinse beans thoroughly with cold water. Place beans in a stainless-steel or porcelain bowl, cover with cold water, and soak overnight. Drain water from beans. Place bacon and beans in a large kettle and cover with water; bring to a boil. Reduce heat and simmer for about 4 hours or until beans are tender. Add salt and stir; cook, uncovered, for 2 hours more or until liquids are almost totally evaporated.

Spinach Salad

- 1½ pounds fresh spinach
- ½ teaspoon garlic, finely minced
- ¼ cup shallots, finely chopped
- 4 slices bacon
- ¼ cup vinegar
- 2 tablespoons peanut oil
- ½ teaspoon salt
- ¼ teaspoon freshly ground black pepper
- ½ teaspoon prepared mustard
- 1 teaspoon sugar
- Croutons

Wash spinach and pat dry. Break spinach into small pieces and place in a large stainless-steel or porcelain bowl; add garlic and shallots, toss lightly and place in refrigerator for 1½ hours.

Fry bacon slices until crisp and drain drippings. Crumble into small pieces. Add vinegar, peanut oil, salt, pepper, mustard, and sugar to bacon; heat thoroughly over low temperature. Pour over chilled spinach, toss lightly with croutons, and serve immediately.

Appendixes

HERBS AND SPICES TO USE WITH WILD GAME AND FISH

ALLSPICE — *boiled fish, oyster stew, turtle soup*
BASIL — *venison, rabbit, duck, mussels, crayfish, shrimp, lobsters, scallops*
BAY LEAVES — *venison, fish chowder, quail, boiled and steamed shrimp*
CARAWAY SEED — *roast goose*
CELERY SEED — *fish and oyster stews, turkey hash, croquettes*
CINNAMON — *boiled fish*
CLOVES — *baked fish, roast sage hens, croquettes*
CUMIN — *fish*
CURRY POWDER — *turkey, hash, croquettes, baked fish, crayfish, shrimp*
DILL — *baked fish, lobster, shrimp, turtle soup*
FENNEL — *boiled fish*
GINGER — *squab, dove*
MARJORAM — *baked and broiled fish, venison, pheasant, duck, goose, stuffing*
MUSTARD — *boiled fish, creamed and stewed oysters, shrimp*
OREGANO — *butter sauce for shellfish, stuffed fish, pheasant*
PARSLEY — *all wild game and fish, stuffing*
ROSEMARY — *venison, quail, pheasant, duck, baked fish*
SAGE — *venison, duck, goose, rabbit, baked fish, turkey, stuffing*
SAVORY — *rabbit and venison stews, duck, turkey, stuffing*
TARRAGON — *duck, turkey, fish, shellfish, fish sauce*
THYME — *venison, stuffing, groundhog, possum, grouse, partridge, pheasant*
TURMERIC — *quail*

Oven Temperatures

Very slow	225 to 250 degrees
Slow	250 to 300 degrees
Moderate	300 to 350 degrees
Moderately hot	350 to 400 degrees
Hot	400 to 450 degrees

Standard Measurements

Dash, pinch, or few grains	less than ⅛ teaspoon
3 teaspoons	1 tablespoon
2 tablespoons	⅛ cup
4 tablespoons	¼ cup
5 tablespoons plus 1 teaspoon	⅓ cup
8 tablespoons	½ cup
10 tablespoons plus 2 teaspoons	⅔ cup
12 tablespoons	¾ cup
16 tablespoons	1 cup
2 cups	1 pint
4 cups or 2 pints	1 quart
4 quarts	1 gallon

Sizes of Cans

No. 1 (16 ounces)	2 cups
No. 2 (20 ounces)	2½ cups
No. 2½ (28 ounces)	3½ cups
No. 3 (32 ounces)	4 cups
No. 10 (104 ounces)	13 cups

Cooking Terms and Definitions

Bake — *To cook by dry heat, usually in an oven.*
Baste — *To ladle water, drippings, or other liquid over food while baking or roasting.*
Batter — *A semiliquid mixture of flour, liquid, and other ingredients thin enough to be poured.*
Beat — *To mix smoothly and lightly with a brisk, even rotary motion.*
Blend — *To combine gently until even and smooth.*
Boil — *To cook in liquid at boiling temperature.*
Braise — *To brown meat in a small amount of fat or salad oil; then to cover and cook slowly in the juices or in a small amount of added liquid.*
Bread — *To cover with fine bread or cracker crumbs before cooking.*
Broil — *To cook by direct heat.*
Chop — *To cut into small, even pieces.*
Coddle — *To cook slowly and gently in a liquid just below the boiling point.*
Combine — *To mix enough to mingle ingredients.*
Cook — *To prepare, using heat.*
Cream — *To make soft, smooth, and creamy.*
Cube — *To cut into even-sided pieces.*
Dice — *To cut into small cubes.*
Dissolve — *To combine a dry and a liquid substance in a solution.*
Dot — *To scatter at random.*
Dough — *A stiffened mixture of flour, liquid and other ingredients thick enough to be kneaded or rolled.*
Dredge — *To coat with a dry substance.*
Dust — *To sprinkle or coat lightly with a dry substance.*
Fold — *To combine, using a motion beginning vertically down through the mixture, continuing across the bottom of the bowl, and ending with an upward and over motion.*
Fry — *To cook in fat or oil until brown and tender.*
Garnish — *To decorate.*
Grate — *To cut into fine pieces by rubbing against a grater.*
Grill — *To cook by direct heat.*

GRIND — *To reduce to small pieces or powder.*
INFUSE — *To steep without boiling.*
JULIENNE — *To cut food into matchlike strips.*
KNEAD — *To roll and press firmly with the heel of the hand.*
MARINATE — *To mix with an oil and acid mixture and chill.*
MASH — *To make soft by pressing.*
MELT — *To heat until liquid.*
MINCE — *To cut or chop very fine.*
MIX — *To combine ingredients until evenly distributed.*
PAN-BROIL — *To cook, uncovered, in hot skillet (ungreased or greased), pouring off fat as it accumulates.*
PARBOIL — *To cook partially or precook in boiling water.*
PARE — *To trim or shave off outer covering.*
PASTE — *A fine, smooth mixture.*
PEEL — *To strip off outer covering.*
PLANK — *To serve on a heavy wooden board made for that purpose.*
PURÉE — *To make a smooth, semiliquid mixture by rubbing through a sieve.*
ROAST — *To cook, uncovered, in the oven without added moisture.*
SAUTÉ — *To cook in a small amount of fat or oil until brown and tender.*
SCALD — *To bring to a temperature just below the boiling point.*
SCORE — *To cut narrow grooves or gashes.*
SHRED — *To cut or tear into thin strips or pieces.*
SIFT — *To put through a fine sieve.*
SIMMER — *To cook in a liquid just below the boiling point.*
SKEWER — *To pierce with, or string on, pointed thin pieces of wood or metal.*
SOFTEN — *To mash until smooth and creamy.*
SPRINKLE — *To dust or coat lightly with a dry substance.*
STEAM — *To cook, covered, over boiling water.*
STEEP — *To extract flavor by soaking in hot liquid.*
STERILIZE — *To free from living microorganisms, as by boiling in water.*
STIR — *To blend ingredients, using circular motions.*
STOCK — *A liquid in which food has been cooked.*

STUFF — *To pack a mixture into a cavity.*
TOAST — *To brown by dry heat.*
TRUSS — *To fasten closely or tightly.*
WHIP — *To incorporate air into a mixture by beating with a brisk, even rotary motion.*

Index

Bass
  beer-fried, 157
  lake, crispy, 156
  striped fillets, wine-baked, 156
  striped, savory baked with piquant sauce, 158
Beans, shuck, about, 195
Bear
  cubes in wine sauce, 64
  dressing and skinning, 9
  hot pot, 62
  steak loaf, rolled, 63
  steak rollups, 61
Birds. See Game birds, names of individual birds: e.g., Dove, Grouse, etc.
Biscuits. See also Bread, Muffins
  baking powder, 189
  buttermilk, 189
  potato, 190
  whole wheat, 190
Bluefish, skipper's baked, 164
Bluegill, baked, 159
Boar, wild, smoked sausage, 35
Bread. See also Biscuits, Muffins
  country corn, 191
  crackling, 191
  Granny's egg, 193

Brunswick stew, 79
Bullfrog. See Frogs' legs

Catfish, baked, 169
Catfish, fried, 168
Clam chowder, 176
Cooking terms and definitions, 199–201
Coon. See Raccoon
Crappie, Cumberland Mountain, fried, 166
Crayfish (crawfish)
  about, 19
  Old Kentucky, creamed, 171
  casserole, creamy, 170
  and mussels, sherried, with brandy sauce, 172

Deer. See Venison
Dove
  about, 19
  baked, and cashew gravy, 132
  and gravy, 134
Drying meat, 36
Duck, wild
  about, 5, 15, 24, 99
  bloody with orange sauce, 103
  breast, barbecued, 106
  breast in wine sauce, 104

Duck, Wild (Cont.)
  herb-fried, 105
  Kentucky-style, 106
  lemon-roast, 102
  liver and savory rattlesnake, 185
  orange-glazed, 104
  pâté, 107
  roast with herbs, 101
  tidbits and rice with sauce, 108
  wine and bourbon, 100

Fish. See also names of individual fish: e.g., Bass, Mackerel, etc.
  about, 18, 22, 28-30
  and chips, 160
  corned, 30
  fillets, almond-baked, 162
  fillets, old Irish casserole, 165
  fillets, poached, 162
  sauce. See Sauces
  smoking, about 31-32
Flounder, broiled spicy, 167
Flounder with wine sauce, 168
Fritters, old-time corn, 193
Frogs' legs
  about, 19
  crispy, 177
  fancy baked, 178
  and sausage, 178

Game animals. See also names of individual animals: e.g., Bear, Raccoon, etc.
  about, 3-6, 22, 25-27
  dressing and skinning, 7-12
Game birds. See also names of individual birds: e.g., Grouse, Pigeon, etc.
  about, 6, 13-15, 24
Game birds, stuffings
  bread, 147
  chestnut and currant, 144
  corn bread, 146

  rice-raisin-almond, 145
  sausage, 144
Goose, wild
  about, 5, 15, 24
  cracklings, 112
  fricasseed, 111
  roast, 110
  smoked, 34
  stuffings
    bread, 147
    chestnut and currant, 144
    corn bread, 146
    fruit, 109
    sausage, 144
Groundhog, braised
  and bourbon sauce, 88
  variations of, 89-90
Groundhog, garlic-flavored fried, 90
Grouse
  with almond and wine sauce, 142
  breast of, 140
  Sage, barbecued, 140
  stuffings
    bread, 147
    chestnut and currant, 144
    corn bread, 146
    sausage, 144

Haddock fillets, poached, 162
Ham, smoked, 35
Hardtack, old-time, 188
Herbs for wild game and fish, 197
Hush puppies, Jennifer's, 192

Mackerel, king, spicy baked, 164
Measurements, standard, 198
Meat, drying, 36
Muffins, pawpaw, 192
Mussels
  about cleaning, 20
  and crayfish, sherried with brandy sauce, 172
  deep-fried, 173

Mussels (Cont.)
  fricassee, 175
  fritters, 174
  oven-fried, 174
  pan-fried, 173
  soup, mountain, 175
Opossum. *See* Possum
Oven temperatures, 198

Partridge, about, 16
Partridge, roast woodbine, 143
Pâtés
  quail, 129; liver, 130
  wild duck, 107
Perch fillets, poached, 162
Pheasant
  about, 16
  barbecued marinated, 113
  breast with mushroom sauce, 116
  raisin-and-pecan stuffing, 114
  roast with vegetables, 115
  sausage stuffing, 144
Pigeon
  about, 5, 17
  potted, 134
Pike, walleyed stuffed, 163
Poke sallet, 194
Possum
  with brandy and wine sauce, 67
  dressing and skinning, 7
  southern baked, 68
Potatoes, home-fried, 194
Ptarmigan
  with orange glaze, 137
  sherried, with pecan dressing, 136

Quail
  about, 17
  Bluegrass with wine sauce, 127
  Bryant County, 128
  famous old-style, 124
  Grandma Rosa's with tomato sauce, 122
  Kentucky stuffed with cream sauce, 118
  little deviled birds, 125
  pâté, 129; liver, 130
  potpie, 126
  roasted, 117
  sauterne, 121
  smoked, 34
  salad, 131
  sandwich, open-faced, 132
  stew, hearty, 130; Brunswick, 79
  stuffings
    corn bread, 146
    Grandma Rose's, 123
    Kentucky dressing, 118
    rice-raisin-almond, 145
  supreme, 120
  with yellow rice, 128

Rabbit
  about, 6
  Brunswick stew, 79
  and cheese casserole, 77
  the colonel's favorite recipe, 74
  coriander and wild rice, 75
  dressing and skinning, 8
  hot spiced, 73
  Italian with almonds, 76
  Kentucky, 69
  lemon-baked, 78
  lemon-broiled, 71
  with mushroom sauce, 70
  oven-fried, crusty, 76
  oven-fried sesame, 74
  pan-fried with country colonel gravy, 70
  sage, 72
  in wine sauce, 72
Raccoon
  Cumberland Valley, 65
  dressings and skinning, 9
  marinated, 66
Rattlesnake
  cocktail, 187
  delight, 187

Rattlesnake (Cont.)
fillets, 184
flambéed, 186
savory, and browned duck liver, 185
steaks, sautéed, 186
Roast. *See* names of individual: e.g., Goose, Venison, etc.

Sage Grouse. *See* Grouse
Salad, spinach, 196
Salmon
baked, 154
boiled with tart sauce, 155
herb-stuffed, 152
stuffed, Melanie Suzanne's, 154
Sauce(s) for
bass, striped, 158
bear cubes, 64
duck, 103, 104, 108
fish and chips, 160-161
flounder, 168
groundhog, 88
grouse, 142
mussels and crayfish, 172
pheasant, 116
possum, 67
quail, 118, 123, 127
rabbit, 70, 72
salmon, 155
squirrel, 80, 81, 84
trout, 152
turkey (smoked), 98
venison, 47, 48
venison meatballs, 55
venison tongue, 59, 60
Shuck beans, 195
Snake, *See* Rattlesnake
Snapper. *See* Turtle
Sole fillets, poached, 162
Spinach salad, 196
Squab
about, 5, 17
Mountain laurel, 135

Squirrel
Brunswick stew, 79
chowder, 86
curried and rice, 82
dressing and skinning, 7
herb-fried, 85
lemon-fried, 83
mountain fried and gravy, 80
in orange sauce, 84; and honey, 81
tasty casserole, 86
in wine sauce, 85
Stew. *See also* names of individual: e.g., Quail, Venison, etc.
Brunswick, 79
Striped bass. *See* Bass.

Terrapin. *See* Turtle
Tomatoes, fried green, 195
Trout
baked in wine sauce, 152
deluxe cheesy, 151
Turkey, wild
about, 6
bread stuffing for, 147
broiled, simple, 97
currant-glazed, 96
dressing, 94
giblet gravy, 94
roast, 93
smoked, 33
smoked, and rice with pineapple sauce, 98
Turtle
about, 20-21
fricassee with wine, 179
snapper, fried succulent, 180
soup, Camp Town, 180
soup, Tennessee, 182
terrapin, Cumberland Mountain, 182
terrapin, Kentucky, 184

Venison
about, 6, 11, 41

Venison (Cont.)
  burgers, Grandma's, 57
  Bryant County, 51
  casserole claret, 52
  chili and beans, Pine Mountain, 56
  chili, Uncle Herbert's secret, 56
  chops in wine, 49
  country-style, 50
  cutlet with apple, 46
  cutlet casserole, 46
  dressing and skinning, 10
  herbed, and mushrooms, 44
  kabobs, barbecued, 54
  liver sautéed with apple slices, 50
  meatballs and wine sauce, 55
  meatloaf, 58
  pot roast, 44
  roast, apple cider, 42
  roast, apple valley, 43
  roast haunch of, tangy, 42
  roast saddle of, 41
  sausage, 58
  steak, broiled with Corbin sauce, 47
  steak, broiled with garlic sauce, 48
  steak, with wine sauce, 48
  stew, orange, 54
  stew, sunset, 53
  tongue, 59
  tongue, tangy sauce for, 60
  tongue, wine sauce for, 59

Walleyed pike, stuffed, 163
Wild birds. *See* Game birds, names of individual birds: e.g., Dove, Quail, etc.
Wild boar smoked sausage, 35
Wild duck. *See* Duck, wild
Wild game. *See* Game animals
Wild goose. *See* Goose, wild
Wild turkey. *See* Turkey, wild
Woodcock
  almond-stuffed, 138
  braised, 139
  rice-raisin-almond stuffing for, 145